主　编◎吴勇毅　　副主编◎刘　弘

School: _____

Grade/Class: _____

Name: _____

China Study

中国研习

刘艳辉　王佳艺◎译

Nicholas Thomas Zazzi ◎审

华东师范大学出版社

·上海·

图书在版编目（CIP）数据

中国研习. 八年级＝China Study. Grade Eight:
汉英对照 / 吴勇毅主编；刘艳辉，王佳艺译. —上海:
华东师范大学出版社, 2019
ISBN 978-7-5675-9869-0

Ⅰ.①中… Ⅱ.①吴… ②刘… ③王… Ⅲ.①汉语—
对外汉语教学—教材 Ⅳ.①H195.4

中国版本图书馆CIP数据核字（2019）第263994号

地图由中华地图学社提供，地图著作权归中华地图学社所有
审图号：GS（2019）4707号

中国研习（八年级）
China Study (Grade Eight)

主　　编　吴勇毅
副 主 编　刘　弘
策划编辑　王　焰
项目编辑　龚海燕　种道旸
责任编辑　顾晨溪
责任校对　曹　勇　时东明
装帧设计　卢晓红

出版发行　华东师范大学出版社
社　　址　上海市中山北路3663号　邮编 200062
网　　址　www.ecnupress.com.cn
电　　话　021-60821666　　行政传真 021-62572105
客服电话　021-62865537　　门市（邮购）电话 021-62869887
地　　址　上海市中山北路3663号华东师范大学校内先锋路口
网　　店　http://hdsdcbs.tmall.com/

印 刷 者　上海邦达彩色包装印务有限公司
开　　本　889×1194　16开
印　　张　13.25
字　　数　153千字
版　　次　2021年9月第1版
印　　次　2021年9月第1次
书　　号　ISBN 978-7-5675-9869-0
定　　价　88.00元

出 版 人　王　焰

（如发现本版图书有印订质量问题,请寄回本社客服中心调换或电话021-62865537联系）

编委会	Editorial Committee

主 编	**Editor-in-Chief**
吴勇毅	WU Yongyi

副主编	**Associate Editor**
刘 弘	LIU Hong

编 委	**Editorial Committee Members**
（按姓名拼音排列）	（Arranged in alphabetical order）
李贞贞	LI Zhenzhen
凌一云	LING Yiyun
邵忆晨	SHAO Yichen
汤莉娜	TANG Lina
吴顺俪	WU Shunli

本册编写人员：	**Contributors of this textbook:**
张季含	ZHANG Jihan
张欣倩	ZHANG Xinqian
张 璐	ZHANG Lu
吴 双	WU Shuang

　　《中国研习》是一套为国际学校1-12年级外籍学生开发的中国文化与社会探究教材。本套教材的编写参考了国际文凭课程（IB课程）大纲，并且吸收了教育部基础教育课程教材发展中心（NCCT）"外籍人员子女学校认证标准"中有关中国文化课程教学的要求。教材采取探究式教学方法，并为该课程研发了数字教育平台，力求创造轻松愉快的学习环境，培养学生开放的、包容的批判性思维能力。

　　全套教材共分成小学、初中和高中三个系列。小学系列共有6册，初中和高中系列各有3册。每册有12个单元，每个单元涉及一个主题，教师可以根据学校的课时安排每周或者若干周学习一个单元，也可以根据教学需要挑选其中某个单元来使用。

　　本套教材具有如下几个主要特点：

1. 以主题方式编写教材

　　主题式教学是以内容为载体、以文本的内涵为主题所进行的一种教学活动。本套教材的主题尽量考虑到国际学校学生在学习、生活中可能会遇到的各种社会文化内容，并且有意识养成学生能对母国文化和中国文化进行比较和思考的习惯，以培养学生的国际情怀。

2. 以探究式活动来组织教材内容编排，便于师生使用

　　中国研习作为一门跨学科探究性课程，兼顾学科内的知识和跨学科领域的知识。为此，本套教材在呈现方式上以探究、活动等多维度方式为主，而非传统的简单的内容灌输施教形式；强调在各种探究活动中帮助学生内化吸收相关的知识和能力，包括不同学科的知识；鼓励学生成为学习的主体，教师则在学生的学习中起到有效的引导作用。

3. 教材所涉及的中国文化和社会的领域十分广泛

为适应国际学校有关中国社会及文化课程的需要，本套教材所涉及的内容不仅仅局限于狭义的中国文化范畴，而是扩展到中国艺术（包括音乐、戏剧、视觉艺术等），政治，经济，历史，地理，科学（包括数学、物理、化学等）等多方面，这与IB课程要跨学科、内容要涉及多种学科领域的理念是一致的。我们认为，中国文化教学不仅是中文教师的工作，其他学科的教师也完全可以参与其中，也唯有如此，才能真正使得文化通识在国际教育环境下扎根。这种跨学科的教学，也符合IB等国际教育中强调的"课程融合"理念。

4. 提供具体的评价指标，便于教师对于学生的表现作出评价

为了适应活动探究的教学需要，本套教材鼓励教师以过程化的档案袋评价方式为主。教师通过对学生在不同阶段的学习过程和学习结果进行评估，及时对学生的学习表现作出反馈并提出改进意见，从而在教学过程中更好地激发学生的兴趣，调动学生的学习主动性，引导他们学习、理解、研究和探索，让学生成为主导自己的主人。

5. 中英文对照编辑，适应多种需要

考虑到国际学校学生汉语水平和课程教学的多样性特点，本套教材采取中英文对照形式，这样既可以满足国际学校基于内容的汉语教学的需要，也可以供国际学校教授其他课程的教师参考或补充教学，还可以作为师生的课外活动手册。此外，教材中将重要文化知识和内容要点列出，也便于学生自学使用。

本套教材的研发团队来自华东师范大学等知名高校和多所国际学校，不仅

包括拥有丰富教学经验和较高理论水平的高校专业教师，还吸收了一部分国际学校一线的教学和管理人员。其核心成员参加过国际汉语教学相关标准、大纲和教材的研发工作，对于各类国际学校常用标准、大纲和课程有过专门研究，在国内外发表过相关的研究成果，具有丰富的课程设计和教材编写经验。

希望通过学习和使用本套教材，能够使更多的国际学生认识中国、了解中国。

吴勇毅

2021 年 9 月

China Study is a set of Chinese culture and social inquiry textbooks designed for foreign students of international schools in grades 1–12. Based on the IB syllabus, this set of textbooks has absorbed the teaching requirements of "certification standards of school for foreign children" developed by National Center for School Curriculum and Textbook Development (NCCT), Ministry of Education. The textbooks adopt an exploration-based teaching method and provide a digital education platform, attempting to create a relaxing and enjoyable learning environment and to develop students' critical thinking skills.

This set of textbooks is divided into three series: elementary school, junior high school and senior high school. There are 6 volumes in the elementary school series and 3 volumes in the junior high school and senior high school series respectively. There are 12 units in each volume and every unit deals with a specific theme. Teachers can teach one unit for each week or several weeks according to class schedule, or select one of the units to use according to requirements.

This set of textbooks has the following main features:

1. Theme-related teaching method

Theme-related teaching method is based on the content and the connotation of each unit. This set of textbooks takes into account the various social and cultural contents that international school students may encounter in their study and life, and intends to cultivate students' habit of comparing and thinking about their native culture and Chinese culture in order to cultivate their international mindedness.

2. Exploratory activities to facilitate teachers' and students' use

China Study is an interdisciplinary exploration course that intends to incorporate knowledge within the discipline and knowledge in interdisciplinary fields. To this end, this set of textbooks is based on exploration, activities and other multi-dimensional ways rather than simply cramming knowledge into students' heads. We emphasize on students' ability to absorb knowledge of different subjects through various exploration activities. We also encourage students to become the initiator of learning and teachers to play an effective guiding role in students' learning.

3. Covering a wide range of Chinese culture and society

In order to meet the needs of the international school curriculum on Chinese society and culture, the content of this set of textbooks is not limited to the narrow Chinese culture category but extended to Chinese art (including music, opera, visual arts, etc.), politics, economy, history, geography, science (including mathematics, physics, chemistry, etc.) and many other aspects—consistent with the concept that IB courses should be interdisciplinary and involve multiple subjects. We believe that Chinese culture teaching is not only the work for Chinese teachers, and teachers from other disciplines can also participate in Chinese culture teaching. Only in this way can cultural education take root in an international education environment. This interdisciplinary teaching is also in line with the "curricular integration" concept emphasized in international education such as IB.

4. Providing specific evaluation means for students' performance

In order to meet the needs of activity exploration, this set of textbooks encourages teachers to focus on process evaluation. Teachers evaluate students' learning process and results at different stages, and give timely feedback and suggestions to students' learning performance so as to evoke students' interest in study and guide them to further understand, research and explore Chinese culture.

5. Editing in both Chinese and English to meet various needs

Taking into consideration the diversity of Chinese language proficiency and curriculum teaching in international schools, this set of textbooks offers both Chinese and corresponding English translations. This can meet the needs of content-based Chinese language teaching in international schools, as well as the needs of international school teachers who teach other courses. It can also be used as a manual for extracurricular activities. In addition, important cultural knowledge and content points are listed in the textbook, which is also convenient for students to study by themselves.

The writers of this set of textbooks come from well-known universities such as East China Normal University (ECNU) and many international schools. They include professional teachers with rich teaching experience and high theoretical level, and also some front-line teaching and management personnel from international schools. Among them, the core members have participated in the development of relevant standards, syllabus and textbooks for international Chinese teaching and have conducted special research on these fields with relevant results published at home and abroad.

We hope that by studying and using this set of materials, more international students can get to know China and understand China better.

September 2021

目录

Contents

第一课 中国茶

1. 学习目标

（1）能说出茶的几种基本类型。

（2）能说明本国人喝茶的特点。

（3）能说明中国人和其他国家的人饮茶习惯的异同。

2. 热身活动

讨论

（1）中国人是从什么时候开始喝茶的？

（2）除了中国人，还有哪些地方的人喜欢喝茶？

（3）你觉得红茶和绿茶有什么不同？在你们国家，人们常喝红茶还是绿茶？

（4）你平时喜欢喝咖啡还是茶？一般什么时候喝？在哪里喝？

（5）你喜欢喝奶茶吗？最近几年中国奶茶店的数量增加很快，你认为造成这一现象的原因有哪些？

3. 阅读课文

中国的茶叶种类

中国茶叶按色泽或制作工艺可分为：绿茶、红茶、白茶、黑茶，另外还有

Lesson One   Chinese Tea

1. Learning objectives

(1) Be able to name several basic types of tea.

(2) Be able to tell the characteristics of drinking tea in one's country.

(3) Be able to explain the similarities and differences of tea-drinking habits between people from China and other countries.

2. Warm-up

Discussion

(1) When did Chinese people start drinking tea?

(2) Besides the Chinese, people from which places like to drink tea?

(3) What do you think are the differences between black tea and green tea? Do people in your country usually drink black tea or green tea?

(4) Which do you prefer, coffee or tea? When and where do you drink it?

(5) Do you like milk tea? In recent years, the number of milk tea shops in China has increased rapidly. What do you think are the reasons?

3. Reading texts

Varieties of Chinese Tea

Chinese tea can be divided into green tea, black tea, white tea, dark tea and

很多的花茶。各种茶叶的产地也不相同。

中国产区最广、产量最大、品质最好的茶类是绿茶，占茶叶总量的70%左右。比较有名的绿茶有西湖龙井、碧螺春等，主要产自浙江、安徽、江苏等地。红茶是中国最重要的出口茶类，主要产自四川、云南、贵州、湖北、湖南等地。白茶主要产自福建。黑茶是中国特有的茶类，常常压制成砖茶、饼茶、沱茶等形状，代表品种是普洱茶，主要产自湖南、湖北、四川、云南、广西等地。花茶是指用植物花、叶、种子、根泡制的草本茶，如菊花茶、枸杞茶、参茶等。

红　茶

世界上最早的红茶出现在中国福建的武夷山茶区，是由当地的茶农发明的。严格说起来，红茶不是指茶的品种，而是一种茶叶的加工工艺。与绿茶有所不同，红茶是一种全发酵性的茶类，是以茶树的芽叶为原料，经过揉捻、发酵、干燥等典型工艺过程精制而成。红茶得名于其干茶色泽和冲泡的茶汤为红色。

various scented tea according to the color and production process. They are also planted in different areas.

Green tea is the most widely grown, most productive, and of the best quality in China. It accounts for about 70% of the total tea production in the country. The famous green tea such as West Lake Longjing tea and Biluochun are mostly produced in Zhejiang, Anhui, and Jiangsu provinces. Black tea, the most important exported tea, is mainly planted in Sichuan, Yunnan, Guizhou, Hubei, and Hunan provinces. White tea is largely produced in Fujian Province. Dark tea, a unique kind of Chinese tea, is often compressed into brick tea, cake tea, bowl-shaped tea, and other shapes, among which Pu'er tea is the best known. It is grown in such provinces like Hunan, Hubei, Sichuan, Yunnan and Guangxi. In addition, there is also scented tea, which is a kind of herbal tea made from flowers, leaves, seeds, or roots of some plants, such as chrysanthemum tea, wolfberry tea, and ginseng tea.

Black Tea

The earliest black tea in the world appeared in the Wuyi Mountain tea area, Fujian Province, China, and was invented by local tea farmers. Strictly speaking, black tea refers to a processing technique for making tea instead of a specific kind of tea. Unlike green tea, black tea is a kind of completely fermented tea, which is refined from the buds and leaves of the tea bush through rolling, fermentation, and drying. Black tea is named for its dry brown color and red brewing soup.

中国人最早喝的茶是绿茶。但绿茶会随着时间而失去味道，红茶能够保存相当长的时间而味道不变，因此红茶能适应长途运输，这也许是红茶传到西方的重要原因之一。

红茶在英国

据记载，欧洲进口红茶的确切时间是1610年。红茶的历史可以追溯到17世纪西方的大航海时代。在过去的几百年中，红茶逐渐成为英国人重要的饮料。

提到英国红茶，就会说到葡萄牙的凯瑟琳公主。她嫁给英国国王查理二世后，便经常在宫中举办茶道表演，这一习惯使中国的红茶开始受到英国上层社

The earliest tea that Chinese people drank was green tea. However, green tea loses its flavor over time while the original taste of black tea can remain for a long time. Therefore, black tea can be transported for a long distance, which may be one of the important reasons why it has spread to the Western countries.

Black Tea in Britain

According to records, the exact year when Europe imported Chinese black tea was 1610. It dates back to the 17th century when the West was in the Age of Exploration. In the past several centuries, black tea has gradually become an important drink to the British.

When it comes to British black tea, we have to mention Princess Catherine of Portugal. After her royal marriage to Charles II of England, she frequently held tea ceremony performances in the palace. This habit made

会的青睐。此后，玛丽二世与安妮女王效仿她在室内摆设中国的陶瓷茶具，并在室内放置中国的屏风，以创造温馨舒适的饮茶氛围。

在这样一种饮茶习惯的影响下，下午茶几乎成了英国民众的"必修课"。不过英国人喝茶的方式与中国人有较大的区别。中国人常常喝清茶，喜欢清新芬芳的自然茶香，而英国人喝起茶来则要复杂许多，他们首先要在茶水中加牛奶和糖，在饮茶之外，还要搭配饼干、糕点等边吃边喝。

逐渐走红的奶茶

中国红茶在西方流行的过程中，不断地适应着西方人的口味，慢慢地发展成为奶茶。此后在中国台湾地区，又有人在西方奶茶的基础上，以独特的配方配制出时尚可口的珍珠奶茶。

在传统出售珍珠奶茶的小店里，没有茶艺师，也没有古色古香的紫砂茶具，而是由服务生上下摇摆着一种不锈钢调酒器，待摇晃出细腻的泡沫后，把起着泡沫的液体注

Chinese black tea become favored by the British upper class. Later, Mary II and Queen Anne followed her example by decorating the interior with Chinese ceramic tea sets and placing Chinese screens to create a cozy atmosphere for drinking tea.

Under the influence of the tea-drinking habit led by the upper class, even the common British people have developed affection towards afternoon tea. However, the way Britons enjoy the tea has hugely diverged from the Chinese methods. The Chinese value the original incense coming naturally from the tea leaves, so they prefer their tea made with pure hot water, while the British prefer a much richer and more complex flavor for their tea. They would add sugar and milk to it, and always prepare cookies and dessert to go with it.

Gradually Popular Milk Tea

In the process of its popularity in the West, Chinese black tea gradually develops into milk tea, with the constantly adaption to Westerners' taste. Since then, some people in Taiwan region have developed a stylish and delicious pearl milk tea based on Western tea with a unique formula.

There are neither tea artists nor antique purple clay tea sets in the shop where pearl milk tea is sold. It's a waiter who swings up and down a stainless steel shaker, pours the foam-rich tea water into the long and tall

入细细长长的高脚杯中，再加入一些冰块和"珍珠"。1990 年起，外带式珍珠奶茶开始流行，经过不断的发展，500 毫升的胶膜封口杯装珍珠奶茶逐渐成为饮料市场上的主流之一。

20 世纪 90 年代，珍珠奶茶登陆中国香港地区，1995 年陆续延伸至中国内地，并逐渐成为年轻人生活中不可缺少的重要组成部分。与需要讲究泡茶、饮茶技术的传统茶道和重视饮茶环境的英式下午茶有所不同，提供外带的珍珠奶茶更好地满足了快节奏都市生活人士的需求。

goblet after the fine foam is shaken, and adds some ice cubes and "pearls". Since 1990, take-away pearl milk tea has come into vogue. With continuous development, 500 ml plastic film-sealed cup of pearl milk tea has gradually become one of the mainstreams in the beverage market.

Pearl milk tea landed in Hong Kong SAR in the 1990s and then spread to Chinese mainland in 1995. Later, pearl milk tea has become an indispensable part of young people's life. The take-away pearl milk tea is different from traditional tea ceremony that requires making and drinking techniques as well as English afternoon tea that emphasizes tea-drinking environment. It better meets the needs of the people with a fast-paced urban life.

4. 重点词汇

走红

珍珠奶茶为什么会**走红**?

咖啡　外带

你会选择在星巴克店里喝**咖啡**还是打包**外带**?

进口

进口的东西一定贵吗?

时髦

你觉得什么地方的人穿着比较**时髦**?

5. 实践活动

（1）奶茶店的特色之一就是"个性化"服务，比如允许顾客选择"少糖""去冰"等选项。请找一家奶茶店，仔细观察该店提供了哪些选项，并且分析一下这家店与其他奶茶店的异同之处。

（2）以小组为单位，对奶茶店的顾客进行采访，问题可以包括平时购买奶茶的频率、喜欢的品牌、青睐的口味等。然后总结一下，为什么现在越来越多的年轻人喜欢喝奶茶。

4. Keywords

become popular

Why is pearl milk tea **becoming popular**?

coffee   take away

Do you choose to have your **coffee** at Starbucks or **take it away**?

import

Are **imported** goods certainly more expensive than native ones?

fashion

Where do you think people dress **fashionably**?

5. Activities

(1) One of the features of the milk tea shop is personalized services, such as allowing customers to choose less sugar or no ice. Find a milk tea shop, and take a close look at the options they offer. Analyze the similarities and differences between this shop and other milk tea shops.

(2) Please interview the customers of the milk tea shop in groups. The questions can include the frequency of buying milk tea, preferred brand and favorite taste, etc. Then summarize why more and more young people like to drink milk tea nowadays.

（3）日本有一种抹茶，看起来和绿茶有些相似，请研究一下抹茶的发展历史以及它和中国绿茶之间的关系。

（4）如果你有机会经营一家茶馆或者奶茶店，你会怎么做来保持其盈利？请从产品设计、经营方式、广告促销、人员管理等方面提出方案。

（5）体验一下中国茶道，并了解一下它和其他国家的茶道有什么异同。

6. 自我评估

	😊	😐	☹
（1）我能说出红茶和绿茶的区别。			
（2）我能比较中西饮茶文化的异同。			
（3）我能根据需求点一杯奶茶。			

(3) There is a matcha in Japan that looks like green tea. Please study the history of matcha and its relationship with Chinese green tea.

(4) If you have the opportunity to run a teahouse or a milk tea shop, what would you do to keep it profitable? Please propose the plan from the aspects of product design, business mode, advertising and promotion, personnel management, and so on.

(5) Experience the Chinese tea ceremony and learn how it is different from the ones of other countries.

6. Self-assessment

	🙂	😐	☹️
(1) I can tell the differences between black tea and green tea.			
(2) I can compare the differences between Chinese tea culture and the Western one.			
(3) I can order a cup of milk tea according to my own needs.			

第二课　支付宝

1. 学习目标

（1）能说明支付宝的常见用途。

（2）能说出支付宝支付与其他支付方式的异同。

（3）能分析支付宝对中国人生活的影响。

2. 热身活动

讨论

（1）你用过支付宝吗？支付宝有哪些功能？

（2）除了支付宝，还有哪些电子支付方式？

（3）支付宝和信用卡有什么异同？

（4）使用信用卡或者手机支付有什么优缺点？

3. 阅读课文

从"淘宝附属"到"独立支付平台"

2004年，阿里巴巴集团创办了独立的第三方支付平台——支付宝，经过十多年的发展，目前支付宝已经成为中国人最重要的网上支付工具之一。

Lesson Two   Alipay

1. Learning objectives

(1) Be able to explain the common use of Alipay.

(2) Be able to talk about the similarities and differences between Alipay and other methods of payment.

(3) Be able to analyze the influence of Alipay on the life of Chinese people.

2. Warm-up

Discussion

(1) Have you used Alipay? What functions does it have?

(2) What are other electronic payment methods besides Alipay?

(3) What are the similarities and differences between Alipay and credit cards?

(4) What are the advantages and disadvantages of paying with credit cards and with mobile phones?

3. Reading texts

From "Taobao Affiliate" to "Independent Payment Platform"

In 2004, Alibaba Group established an independent third-party payment platform, Alipay. After more than ten years of development, Alipay has become one of the most important online payment methods for Chinese people.

　　支付宝最开始是作为淘宝网的附属品出现的，主要是为了解决网购支付的安全问题。买家在淘宝网或者其他购物平台选好物品后，点击"立即购买"按钮进入订单确认环节，在确定好收货信息后，"提交订单"，输入密码，买方完成支付。此时钱款并未直接打入卖家账户，而是进入支付宝平台。在买家收到物品，"确认收货"之后，支付宝平台将钱款汇入卖家账户。在此过程中，支付宝承担着"交易中介"的角色，起到"担保交易"的作用，降低了淘宝购物的风险。

　　随着淘宝的快速发展，阿里巴巴逐渐意识到支付宝的重要作用。2004年12月，支付宝从淘宝中分离出来，成为一个独立的支付平台。这之后，支付宝的业务范围一步步扩大，到今天已经包含电子商务、生活缴费、财富管理、购物娱乐、教育公益以及第三方服务等诸多应用在内，服务于人们的日常生活。

At the very beginning, Alipay was an affiliate of Taobao, mainly aimed at solving the security problem of online shopping payment. After the consumers select the items on Taobao or other shopping platforms, they click the "Buy Now" button to enter the order confimation link. After confirming the payment information, they submit the order, enter the password, and complete payment. At this point, the payment does not directly enter the seller's account, but enters the Alipay platform. After the buyer receives the item and confirms the delivery, the Alipay platform transfers the payment to the seller's account. In this process, Alipay plays the role of "transaction intermediary", which guarantees the transaction reducing the risk of shopping on Taobao.

As the business of Taobao grows rapidly, Alibaba had gradually become aware of the importance of Alipay. In December 2004, Alipay was spun off from Taobao and became an independent payment platform. Since then, Alibaba has expanded its business step by step. Today, it meets people's daily needs in various aspects including e-commerce, utility payment, wealth management, shopping and entertainment, education and public welfare, the third party services, etc.

支付宝用途花样多

支付宝有很多功能，下面介绍常用的三种功能。

第一是支付。支付宝作为一个支付平台，最重要的任务是帮助人们快捷、方便、安全地完成支付过程。为了更好地完成这项使命，支付宝率先推出"扫码支付"。在中国的大街小巷，无论是小摊贩还是大的超市、商场，在结账的地方总摆放或粘贴着一个二维码，当顾客选择用支付宝支付时，收银员会告诉顾客应付的金额，并让顾客扫此二维码，在顾客输入付款密码后，就完成了一次扫码支付。另一种扫码的方式是，由顾客出示自己用来支付的二维码，收银员用专业的扫码器进行扫描，"滴"的一声之后，扣款就完成了，顾客可在手机上查看付款的金额。扫码支付高效、便捷。目前在中国，这种支付形式最常见。

第二是理财。支付宝有一个小应用，叫作"余额宝"。它于2013年出现，帮支付宝开拓了理财业务。到目前为止，余额宝已经是中国最大的货币基金。余额宝为何会受人们的喜爱呢？首先是因为操作简单、方便安全。只要下载了支付宝客户端，开通了余额宝业务，人们就可以把资金转到余额宝中。转入资金没有最低限制，即使只有一元、两元，人们也可以享受到理财的乐趣。余额宝对转入的资金进行管理，一旦被盗，用户将得到全额补偿。同时，余

Various Functions of Alipay

Alipay has many functions. The most common three are as follows:

The first is payment. As a payment platform, Alipay's essential task is to help people pay in a quick, convenient, and safe way. To better achieve this goal, Alipay is the first to introduce "Payment via Barcode / QR Code". A QR code is always provided at the checkout in supermarkets and shopping malls, or at small stores and even street vendors in back alleys. If a customer chooses to pay with Alipay, the cashier will tell him/her the amount of the payment and ask him/her to scan the QR code. Then, the payment is made after the customer enters the password. There is an alternative to the above method. After the customer shows his/her own QR code, the cashier scans it with a QR code scanner. Then, the payment is made after the "beep" and the customer can check the amount of the payment on his/her phone. "Payment via Barcode / QR Code" is so efficient and convenient that it has become the most common way of payment in China.

The second is wealth management. Alipay has a small application called "Yu'E Bao". It appeared in 2013 and helped Alipay open up its wealth management business. Up to now, Yu'E Bao has become China's largest monetary fund. Why do people favor Yu'E Bao? First of all, it is convenient, safe, and easy to be operated. As long as people download the Alipay App, open the business of Yu'E Bao, they can transfer money to Yu'E Bao. There is no minimum requirement for the sum transferred, even if people only have one or two yuan. Therefore, people can enjoy the pleasure in managing wealth. Yu'E Bao manages the transferred funds, and in case the money is stolen, the user

额宝中资金的使用非常灵活，人们可以直接用余额宝中的资金进行支付，这就意味着我们的钱一方面可以时时保持增值，另一方面又可以随时用来消费。

　　支付宝也参与公益活动。这方面的代表是支付宝里面的"蚂蚁森林"。人们可以在支付宝里"种树"，还可以摘取小伙伴的"绿色能量"。这些都是蚂蚁森林提供的活动。支付宝在消费者同意的情况下，会追踪用户的步行或骑自行车足迹，兑换成绿色能量。用户可以搜集自己的绿色能量，也可以搜集支付宝好友的绿色能量。搜集到的能量用来"浇树"。当你在虚拟的世界里养成一棵树的时候，公益组织将在现实世界为你种下一颗真正的树。截至2018年上半年，"蚂蚁森林"已经播种了5,552万棵树，保护了中国3.9万平方公里的土地，总共减少了超过200万吨的碳排放量。

| ‹ 首页 | Q 全部应用 |

为你推荐

| 车问题全搞定 | 全球付汇率优 | 我的小程序 |
| 车主服务 | 汇率换算 | 小程序收藏 |

便民生活　　财富管理　　资金往来　　购物娱乐

充值中心	信用卡还款	生活缴费	城市服务
我的快递	医疗健康	记账本	发票管家
车主服务	交通出行	体育服务	安全备忘

财富管理

| 余额宝 | 花呗 | 芝麻信用 | 借呗 |
| 保 | ¥ | | |

will receive full compensation. Also, it's very flexible for people to use the funds in Yu'E Bao. People can pay directly with the money in Yu'E Bao, which means they can increase the value of their funds and at the same time use it as payment.

In addition, Alipay takes part in charity activities. One of the typical examples is its "Ant Forest". People can "plant trees" and sometimes collect their friends' "green energy", which are the activities the "Ant Forest" offers. Furthermore, with the permission of the clients, Alipay follows the tracks of their walking or riding bicycle, which can be converted into "green energy". In these ways, the clients can either collect their own "green energy" or that of their friends. The energy collected is used to "water trees". When you successfully grow a tree in the virtual world, a real tree will be planted somewhere chosen in the real world by a charity organization. By the end of the first half of 2018, "Ant Forest" had planted 55,520,000 trees. These trees have protected 39,000 square kilometers of China's land and decreased over 2,000,000 tons of carbon emission in total.

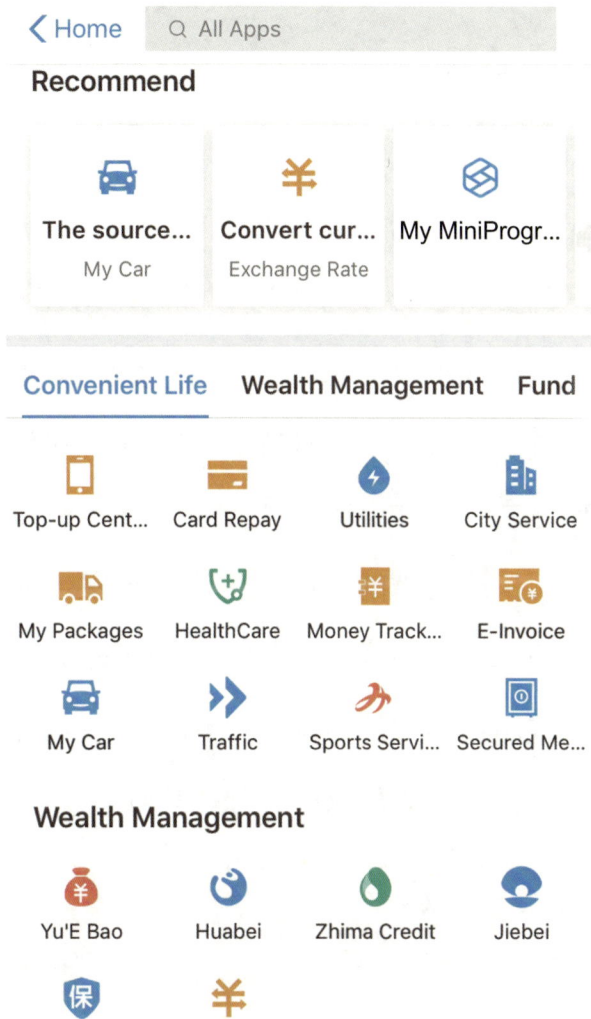

支付宝与微信支付的激烈竞争

微信支付是由腾讯公司推出的一款附属于微信的线上支付工具，通过微信App可以完成缴费、充值、转账等操作，是除支付宝外，另一种常见的支付方式。微信支付依赖于微信使用者，为广大顾客提供了转账、红包、刷卡支付、扫码支付、公众号支付等服务，旨在满足微信用户的社交性支付。相比之下，支付宝作为一个专门的支付平台，提供了包括快捷支付、信用卡支付、余额宝支付、花呗支付、消费卡支付等多种支付方式，旨在满足顾客全面的支付需要。除此之外，微信支付和支付宝都有许多线上应用。支付宝将线上应用分为六大类，从最基础的"便民生活"出发，依次包括"财富管理""资金往来""购物娱乐""教育公益"和"第三方服务"等，种类丰富，布局严谨。微信支付的线上应用包括"腾讯服务"和"第三方服务"两大类，满足人们最基本的生活需要。总之，这两种支付方式各具特色、竞争激烈。

4. 重点词汇

支付宝

你常用**支付宝**做什么？

The Fierce Competition Between Alipay and WeChat Pay

WeChat Pay is an online payment tool affiliated with WeChat. Payment, recharge, and transfer can be operated on WeChat App. Following Alipay, WeChat Pay has now become another common way of payment. WeChat users are the clients of WeChat Pay. To satisfy the need for payment on social platforms, WeChat Pay offers various services, such as transferring money, sending money in red envelopes, paying by cards, paying by scanning codes, and paying official accounts. Compared with it, Alipay is a professional payment platform to satisfy the clients' every need for payment. It offers several payment methods including quick pay, pay by credit cards, Yu'E Bao, Huabei, pay by consumer cards, etc. Moreover, both WeChat Pay and Alipay have various online applications. Alipay's applications fall into 6 categories including "Convenient Life", followed by "Wealth Management", "Fund Transfer", "Shopping & Entertainment", "Education & Public Welfare", and "Third-Party Services", ranging from the most basic to the most advanced ones. The online application of WeChat Pay mainly includes two types, "Tencent Service" and "Third-Party Service", which satisfy the fundamental needs of people in daily life. In a word, each of these two payment tools has its own characteristics, which results in a fierce competition between them.

4. Keywords

Alipay

What do you usually do with **Alipay**?

二维码

二维码在你们国家怎么说？

微信

在你们国家有没有类似**微信**的应用软件？

第三方支付平台

在你们国家，人们常用的**第三方支付平台**有哪些？

余额宝

余额宝有什么好处？

密码

你会用生日作为**密码**吗？

蚂蚁森林

支付宝为什么要开发"**蚂蚁森林**"这个功能？

5. 实践活动

（1）在很多国家，无纸化支付的主流形式是信用卡，电子支付在这些国家发展不如中国那么迅速。请和同学一起分析一下，为什么电子支付会在中国这么快地发展起来？

（2）请查阅资料，比较一下支付宝和PayPal的异同。

（3）在中国，与支付宝类似的还有微信支付，请列表比较它们在支付方式

QR code

What's the word for **QR code** in your country?

WeChat

Do you have applications simiar to **WeChat** in your country?

third-party payment platform

What **third-party payment platforms** do people usually use in your country?

Yu'E Bao

What are the advantages of **Yu'E Bao**?

password

Do you use birthday date as your **password**?

Ant Forest

Why did Alipay develop the **Ant Forest**?

5. Activities

(1) Credit card is the main paperless way of payment in many countries. However, electronic payment has not developed as fast in these countries as in China. Discuss with your classmates and analyze the reasons.

(2) Do some research, and then tell the similarities and differences of Alipay and PayPal.

(3) In China, WeChat Pay is a similar payment tool to Alipay. Compare and

和特点方面的异同。

（4）支付宝和微信除了有支付功能外，还有很多其他功能，比如支付宝还可以帮助人们查询公交信息等。这种融多个功能于一体的App的设计思想是什么？其他国家常见的则是不同的App发挥不同的功能，支付宝同这类App相比，有什么优缺点？

（5）使用支付宝等电子支付时候，应如何保证安全性？支付宝有哪些措施来保证使用的安全？

（6）支付宝给人们的生活带来了很多便利，但是与此同时也出现了一些支付宝盗刷案件。假如你的支付宝被盗刷了，你该怎么办？

（7）有人发现，以支付宝为代表的电子货币会驱动消费者更喜欢提前消费或透支消费，未来人们的负债情况可能会比较严重。对此你认同吗？我们是否应该因此而少用或不用支付宝呢？请给出你的建议。

6. 自我评估

	☺	😐	☹
（1）我会使用支付宝。			
（2）我能说出支付宝的主要功能。			
（3）我能说明支付宝和微信支付的区别。			

list their similarities and differences in terms of features and methods of payment.

(4) Alipay and WeChat have other functions besides making payment. For example, Alipay helps people check public transit information. What is the design concept of such a multi-functional App? On the other hand, it is common in other countries that different Apps have different functions. Compared with those Apps, what advantages and disadvantages does Alipay have?

(5) What should be done to guarantee the security for electronic payment such as Alipay? What has Alipay done to guarantee its payment security?

(6) Alipay has brought convenience to people's life. On the other hand, there are cases of unauthorized payment reported. What would you do if an unauthorized charge is made on your Alipay account?

(7) It has been found that electronic money such as Alipay drives people to consume in advance or even over consume. Probably, more people will be in debt in the future. Do you think so? Should we use less or stop using Alipay? Put forward your suggestions.

6. Self-assessment

	☺	😐	☹
(1) I know how to use Alipay.			
(2) I can list the main functions of Alipay.			
(3) I can tell the differences between Alipay and WeChat Pay.			

第三课　数学之美

1. 学习目标

（1）了解中心对称、轴对称的基本概念。

（2）能说明中心对称、轴对称在生活中的应用。

（3）能说明建筑中的数学之美。

2. 热身活动

讨论

（1）平移、中心对称和轴对称是什么意思？

（2）京剧中的脸谱有什么特点？

（3）看看中国的古代建筑，比如故宫，分析它的特点。

（4）你知道黄金分割吗？生活中有哪些地方体现了黄金分割的应用？

3. 阅读课文

中心对称和轴对称

在平面内，如果把一个图形绕某个点旋转180°后，能与另一个图形重合，那么就说这两个图形关于这个点成中心对称。这样的图形就是中心对称图形。

Lesson Three   The Beauty of Mathematics

1. Learning objectives

(1) Understand the basic concepts of centrosymmetry and axisymmetry.

(2) Be able to explain the applications of centrosymmetry and axisymmetry in life.

(3) Be able to explain the beauty of mathematics in architecture.

2. Warm-up

Discussion

(1) What do translation, centrosymmetry, and axisymmetry mean?

(2) What are the characteristics of facial makeups in Peking Opera?

(3) Look at ancient Chinese architecture, such as the Forbidden City, and analyze its characteristics.

(4) Do you know the golden section? What parts of life reflect the application of golden section?

3. Reading texts

Centrosymmetry and Axisymmetry

In a plane, if a figure rotates 180 degrees around one point and can coincide with another figure, the two figures are said to be central of symmetry with

下面这个阴阳的符号就是中心对称图形。

如果一个平面图形沿着一条直线折叠后，直线两旁的部分能够互相重合，那么这个图形叫作轴对称图形，这条直线叫作对称轴。下面这个双喜字就是典型的轴对称图形。

respect to this point. Such a figure is a centrosymmetric figure. The symbol of *yin* and *yang* below is a centrosymmetric figure.

If a plane figure folds along a straight line and the parts on both sides of the line coincide with each other, the figure maintains an axisymmetric symmetry, and the line is called an axis of symmetry. The following double-happiness character is a typical axisymmetric figure.

脸谱中的轴对称

轴对称图形中，如果我们把图案沿着对称轴翻折，左右两边就能够完全重合。由于对称的物体常常给人一种均衡、庄严的感觉，给人美的感受，因此经常被用在各种艺术设计作品中。在日常生活中，轴对称的物品处处可见，比如风筝、脸谱等。

Axisymmetry in Facial Makeups in Peking Opera

In an axisymmetric figure, if we flip the pattern along the axis of symmetry, the left and right sides can completely coincide. Because symmetrical objects often give people a sense of balance and dignity, along with a sense of beauty, they are often used in various works of art and design. Axisymmetric objects can be seen everywhere in life, such as kites and facial makeups.

如果我们已经知道了一条直线和一个已知图形，如何根据这些条件做出已知图形关于这条直线的轴对称图形呢？可以按照以下步骤来做：

步骤一：过已知的一个点A做一条垂直于已知直线l的直线l′。

步骤二：用圆规截取点A到已知直线l的距离。

步骤三：以垂足为圆心，点A到已知直线l的距离为半径画弧，与直线l′交于点B。

那么点B就是点A的对称点。接着依次把这个图形的关键点都找出来，连起来就是原图形的轴对称图形。

因此，看上去有些复杂的脸谱图案其实并没有那么难完成，如果你对京剧脸谱很感兴趣，不如尝试着运用轴对称设计一个属于自己的脸谱吧。

中国著名建筑中的数学美

人们在日常生活中随处可见各种建筑，其实建筑设计中广泛应用了数学。让我们一起来看看中国建筑里的数学美吧！

（1）赵州桥

仔细观察，可以发现河北省赵县的赵州桥有一个轴对称的单孔石拱桥。这种设计由于没有桥墩，既增强了排水功能，又方便舟船往来。石拱的跨度为

If we know a straight line and a known figure, how can we make an axisymmetric figure of the known figure about the straight line according to these conditions? The following steps can be taken:

Step 1: Make a Line l' perpendicular to the known Line l through a known Point A.

Step 2: Use a pair of compasses to intercept the distance from Point A to the known Line l.

Step 3: Draw an arc with the vertical foot as the center, the distance from Point A to the known Line l as the radius, and intersect with Line l' at Point B.

So Point B is the symmetric point of Point A. Then the key points of the figure are found out in turn. Connect these points with line segments and the axisymmetric figure of the original figure appears.

Therefore, it seems that some complex facial makeup patterns are not so difficult to complete. If you have interest, try to use axisymmetry to design one of your own.

Mathematical Beauty in Famous Chinese Architecture

People can see various buildings in their daily life. Actually, mathematics is widely used in architectural design. Let's take a look at some buildings in China that are full of mathematical beauty.

(1) Zhaozhou Bridge

Careful observation shows that Zhaozhou Bridge in Zhaoxian County, Hebei Province has an axisymmetric single-hole stone arch bridge. Because there are no piers, it not only increases the drainage function, but also facilitates the

37.37米，连南北桥堍（桥两头靠近平地处），总共长50.82米。采取这样的巨型跨度，在当时是一个空前的创举。石拱跨度很大，但拱矢（桥洞的高度）只有7.23米。拱矢和跨度的比例大约是1∶5。可见桥高比拱弧的半径要小得多，整个桥身只是圆弧的一段。

（2）湖南长沙龙王港中国结大桥——莫比乌斯带和中国结

湖南长沙龙王港设计的人行桥梁以莫比乌斯带为原型，还融入了中国结元素。其独特的莫比乌斯带（中国结）造型为坚固的桥梁注入柔美气质，好像缎带一样优美柔和的人行桥，仿佛舞者的水袖掠过梅西河。设计采用多种工艺，行人可在不同高度选取路线过桥。

passage of boats. The span of the stone arch is 37.37 meters. It connects the north and south bridgeheads (the two ends of the bridge near the flat ground), totalling 50.82 meters. Taking such a huge span was an unprecedented initiative at that time. The stone arch has a long span, but the rise of the arch (the height from the two feet of the stone arch to the vault) is only 7.23 meters. The rise-to-span ratio is about 1 to 5. It can be seen that the height of the bridge is much shorter than the radius of the arch, and the whole bridge body is only a section of the arc.

(2) Longwanggang Chinese Knot Bridge in Changsha, Hunan Province—Mobius Strip and Chinese Knots

The pedestrian bridge in Longwanggang, Changsha, Hunan Province is built based on the Mobius strip and incorporates Chinese knots. Its unique Mobius strip (Chinese knot) shape injects a soft temperament into the solid bridge, like a beautiful and soft footbridge of ribbon, and like the sleeves of dancers across the Meixi River. The design adopts a variety of techniques and pedestrians can choose different routes at different heights to cross the bridge.

（3）广州电视塔——单页双曲面

广州电视塔（"小蛮腰"）的外型是典型的单页双曲面，即直纹面。单页双曲面的每条母线都是直线，通俗来说，虽然看上去广州电视塔外边是光滑的曲线，中间细两头宽，但是事实上每一根柱子自下而上都是直的，所以广州电视塔是一堆笔直的柱子斜着搭起来的！

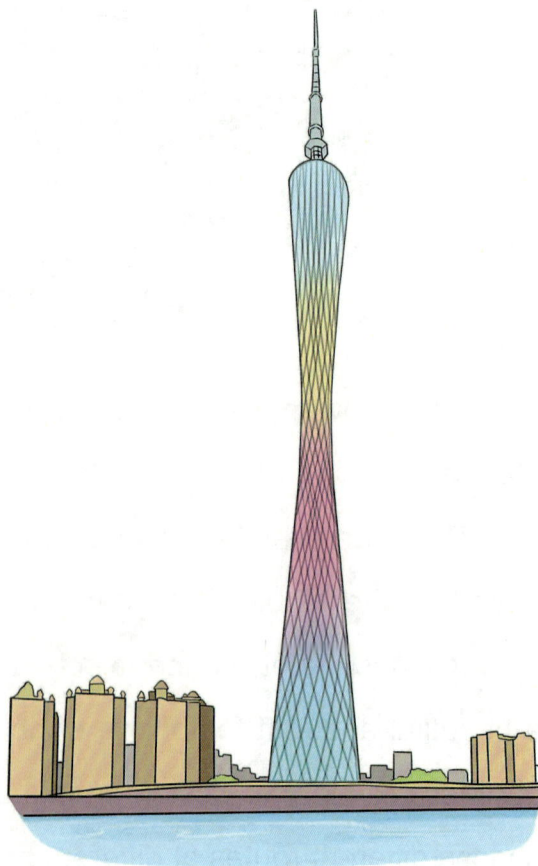

(3) Guangzhou TV Tower—The Hyperboloid of One Sheet

The appearance of Guangzhou TV Tower ("slim waist") is a typical hyperboloid of one sheet, i.e. a ruled surface. Every generatrix of a one-sheeted hyperboloid is a straight line. Generally speaking, although it seems that the outside of Guangzhou TV Tower is a smooth curve and the middle is thin and two ends wide, in fact, every column is straight from bottom to top. Therefore, Guangzhou TV Tower is a bunch of straight columns slanted together.

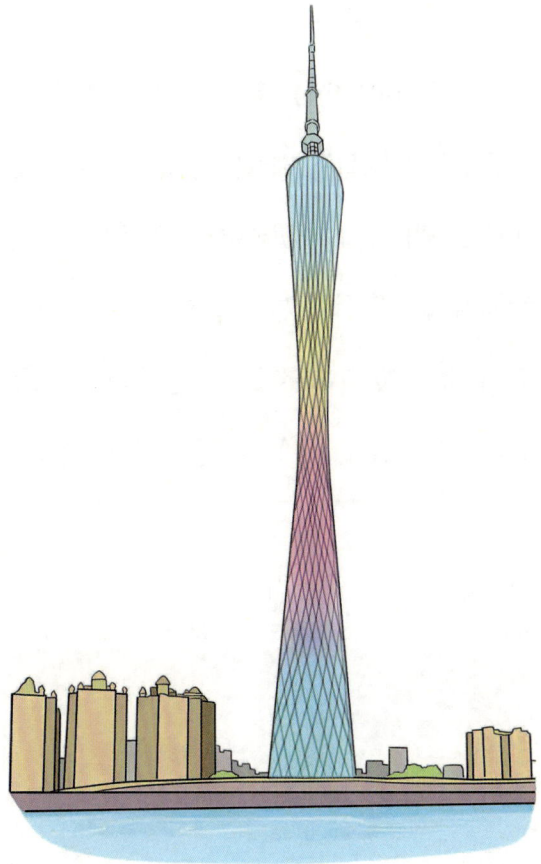

（4）上海东方明珠电视塔——黄金分割比

尽管东方明珠电视塔从几何组成上看十分单调，而且完整的圆形或球形在画面中似乎也比较抢眼，但是设计师在这个建筑中多处运用了黄金分割的比例，使其协调美观。此外，它的三个圆球包含了"大珠小珠落玉盘"的艺术理念。东方明珠电视塔是前往上海旅游观光的人们的必到之地。

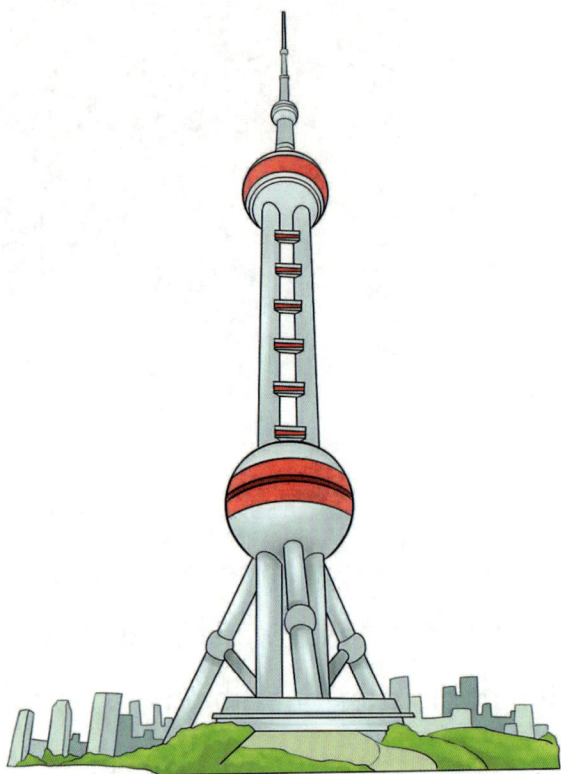

（5）故宫——对称

故宫的建筑严格遵循对称规则，沿一条南北走向的中轴线排列。这些建筑都坐北朝南，体现着皇帝的尊严。中轴两端的建筑阴阳对称。中轴即是中央子午线，是规划故宫全部宫殿及北京城的基准线。故宫内的朝政三大殿，即奉天殿、华盖殿、谨身殿（后改名为太和殿、中和殿、保和殿）和后寝三宫（乾清宫、交泰宫、坤宁宫）均位于中轴线上。

(4) Shanghai Oriental Pearl TV Tower—Golden Ratio

The Oriental Pearl TV Tower is very monotonous in terms of geometric composition, and the complete circle or sphere seems to be more eye-catching in the picture. However, the designer uses the golden ratio in many parts of the building to make it harmonious and beautiful. What's more, the three spheres contain the artistic concept of "big pearls and small pearls falling on the jade plate". The Oriental TV Pearl Tower is a must-see place for tourists in Shanghai.

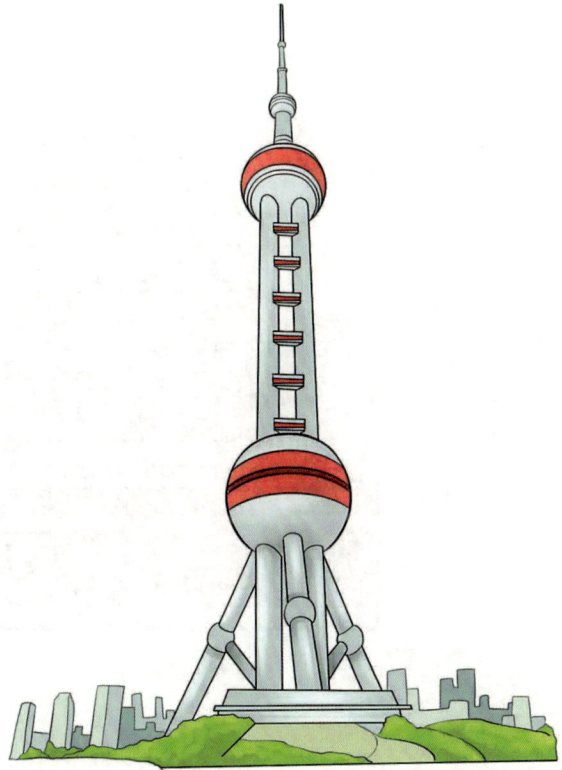

(5) The Forbidden City—Symmetry

The buildings of the Forbidden City strictly follow the symmetrical rules and are arranged along a north-south axis. These buildings are all facing south, reflecting the dignity of the emperor. The buildings at both ends of the central axis are symmetrical in *yin* and *yang*. The central axis is the central meridian, which is the baseline for planning all palaces of the Forbidden City and Beijing City. The three palaces of court administration in the Forbidden City, namely Fengtian Palace, Huagai Palace, Jinshen Palace (later renamed as Taihe Palace, Zhonghe Palace, Baohe Palace) and the three sleeping quarters (Qianqing Palace, Jiaotai Palace and Kunning Palace) are all located

其他宫殿若不建在中轴线上，也是严格按照对称规则进行布局，分布在中轴线两端。

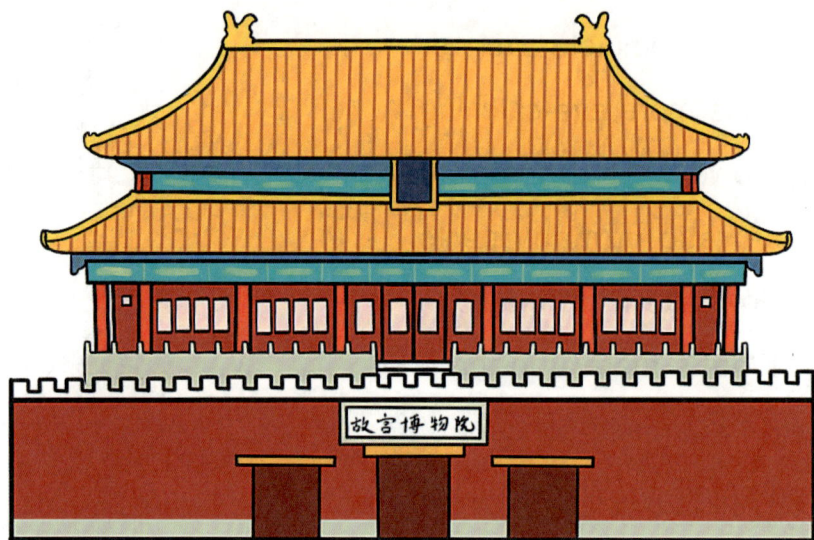

北京中轴线

北京中轴线，是指北京自元大都、明清北京城以来北京城市东西对称布局建筑物的对称轴，北京市诸多其他建筑物都位于这条轴线上。明清北京城的中轴线南起永定门，北至钟鼓楼，直线距离长约7.8公里。

20世纪90年代，北京为连接城市中心和亚运村，在二环路钟鼓楼桥引出鼓楼外大街，向北至三环后改名为北辰路，这条路成为北京中轴线的延伸，西边

on the central axis. Other palaces, even if they are not built on the central axis, are also strictly arranged according to symmetrical rules and distributed at both sides of the central axis.

The Central Axis of Beijing

The central axis of Beijing refers to the symmetrical axis of buildings with a symmetrical east-west layout in Beijing since the Yuan, Ming, and Qing Dynasties. Many other buildings in Beijing are also located on this axis. The central axis of Beijing in Ming and Qing Dynasties starts from Yongding Gate in the south and goes north to Bell Tower and Drum Tower. The straight-line distance is about 7.8 kilometers.

In the 1990s, in order to connect the city center with the Asian Games Village, Beijing introduced the Zhongguwai Street at Zhonggulou Bridge on the Second Ring Road and renamed as Beichen Road after going north to the Third

建造中华民族园，东边则是国家奥林匹克体育中心。

北京申奥成功后，中轴线再次向北延长，成为奥林匹克公园的轴线。东边建造国家体育场（鸟巢），西边则是国家游泳中心（水立方）。再向北，穿过奥林匹克公园，到达奥林匹克森林公园，该公园中间的仰山、奥海均在中轴线上。

2018年7月，北京中轴线申遗已确定天安门等14处遗产点。

4. 重点词汇

轴对称

生活中哪些地方能看到**轴对称**图形？

设计　建筑

你知道哪些著名的建筑设计师？他们**设计**了什么**建筑**？

黄金分割

生活中哪些地方能看到**黄金分割**的应用？

电视塔

你生活的城市有**电视塔**吗？有多高？

Ring Road. This road became an extension of the central axis of Beijing, with the construction of the Chinese National Park in the west and the National Olympic Sports Center in the east.

After Beijing's successful bid for the Olympic Games, the central axis of the Olympic Park has been extended northward again. The National Stadium (Bird's Nest) is built in the east and the National Swimming Center (Water Cube) in the west. Then it stretches to the north, through the Olympic Park, to the Olympic Forest Park, in which Yangshan and the Aohai Lake are both on the central axis.

In July 2018, 14 heritage sites such as Tian'anmen Square have been identified for the application of the central axis of Beijing.

4. Keywords

axisymmetry

Where can you see **axisymmetric** figures in your life?

design building

What famous architects do you know? What **buildings** did they **design**?

golden section

Where can you see the application of **golden section** in your life?

TV Tower

Is there a **TV Tower** in the city where you live? How high is it?

5. 实践活动

（1）跟同学一起讨论一下：还有哪些图形是轴对称图形？有几条对称轴？

（2）0和8有几条对称轴？

（3）看一下红领巾、量角器、黑板、桌面、电视机的图片，讨论一下这几个轴对称图形的对称轴。

（4）查找资料，向同学介绍建筑设计中与数学相关的元素，需要具体说明平移、旋转、轴对称数学元素在建筑中的表现。

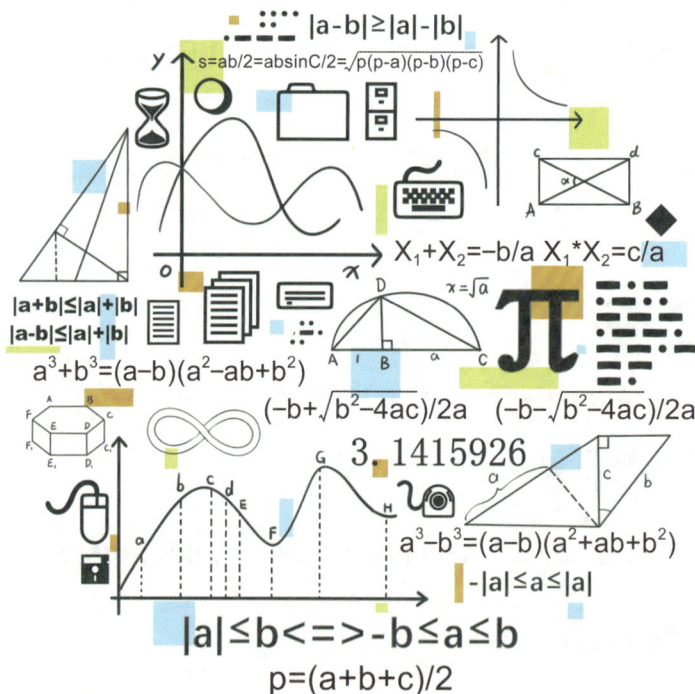

（5）你们国家是否有与数学有关的小游戏？如果有的话，请把规则教给你的同学，一起玩一玩。

5. Activities

(1) Discuss with your classmates the following two questions: What other figures are axisymmetric? How many symmetrical axes are there?

(2) How many symmetrical axes do 0 and 8 have?

(3) Look at the pictures of the red scarf, protractor, blackboard, desktop and TV, and discuss the symmetrical axis of these axisymmetrical figures.

(4) Search for material and introduce mathematics-related elements in architectural design to your classmates. Specify the applications of translation, rotation, and axisymmetric in architecture.

$$|a-b| \geq |a|-|b|$$

$$s = ab/2 = ab\sin C/2 = \sqrt{p(p-a)(p-b)(p-c)}$$

$$X_1 + X_2 = -b/a \quad X_1 * X_2 = c/a$$

$$x = \sqrt{a}$$

$$|a+b| \leq |a|+|b|$$
$$|a-b| \leq |a|+|b|$$
$$a^3 + b^3 = (a-b)(a^2 - ab + b^2)$$

$$(-b + \sqrt{b^2 - 4ac})/2a \quad (-b - \sqrt{b^2 - 4ac})/2a$$

$$3.1415926$$

$$a^3 - b^3 = (a-b)(a^2 + ab + b^2)$$

$$-|a| \leq a \leq |a|$$

$$|a| \leq b <=> -b \leq a \leq b$$

$$p = (a+b+c)/2$$

(5) Do you have any mathematics-related games in your country? If so, please teach the rules to your classmates and play together.

6. 自我评估

	☺	😐	☹
（1）我能说明中心对称、轴对称等词的意义。			
（2）我能说出轴对称图形在生活中的表现。			
（3）我会玩两三个中国传统的数学游戏。			

6. Self-assessment

	🙂	😐	☹️
(1) I can explain the meaning of centrosymmetry and axisymmetry.			
(2) I can illustrate the applications of axisymmetric figures in life.			
(3) I can play two to three traditional Chinese math games.			

第四课　中国的住宅

1. 学习目标

（1）能说明北京四合院的建筑特点。

（2）能说明上海石库门的建筑特点。

（3）知道汉语中街、弄、巷的意思。

（4）了解中国人的购房观念。

2. 热身活动

讨论

（1）你生活中看到的中国的住宅跟你们国家的有没有差异？具体表现在哪些方面？

（2）中国人住的房子有什么特点？

（3）在你们国家，100年以前的房子和现在的有什么异同？

（4）如果你将要自己设计一座房子，你会怎么设计？

Lesson Four　Chinese Houses

1.　Learning objectives

(1)　Be able to explain the architectural characteristics of Beijing courtyard buildings.

(2)　Be able to explain the architectural characteristics of the Shikumen buildings in Shanghai.

(3)　Know the meanings of streets, lanes, and alleys in Chinese.

(4)　Understand the Chinese people's concept of buying houses.

2.　Warm-up

Discussion

(1) Are there any differences between the Chinese houses you see in your life and those in your country? What are the differences?

(2)　What are the characteristics of Chinese houses?

(3)　In your country, what are the similarities and differences between the houses of 100 years ago and those of today?

(4)　If you are going to design a house by yourself, how would you design it?

3. 阅读课文

北京的四合院

中国传统住宅建筑中特别有名的是北京的四合院。所谓四合，"四"指东、西、南、北四面，"合"即四面房屋围在一起，形成一个"口"字形。明清时期，皇帝居住的故宫就是一个四合院，只不过它特别大。四合院可分为中庭院、垂门、桥廊、厢房等，不同的房间有着各自的功能。四合院中，一般主房坐北朝南，房屋地基较高，是主人的居室。两侧厢房一般是子女的住所。下房则主要放置杂物，少数也作为厨房。一家老少，从上到下，均按照辈分来分配居室。封闭式的住宅使四合院具有很强的私密性。关起门来自成天地，院内则四面房门都开向院落，十分适宜居住。

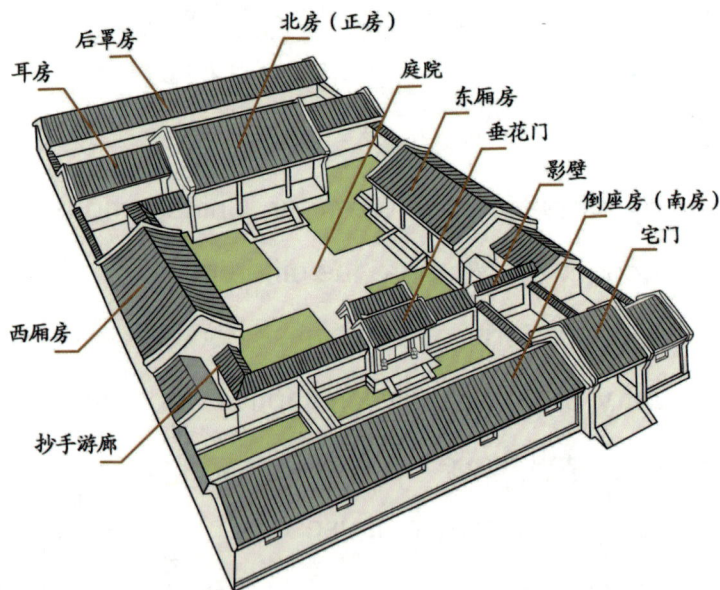

后罩房　　北房（正房）
耳房　　　　　　庭院
　　　　　　东厢房
　　　　　　　垂花门
　　　　　　　　影壁
　　　　　　倒座房（南房）
　　　　　　　宅门
西厢房
抄手游廊

3. Reading texts

The Courtyard Buildings in Beijing

Among the traditional Chinese residential buildings in China, the courtyard buildings (literally meaning four-in-one buildings) in Beijing are very famous. The so-called "four" refers to the east, west, south, and north, and the "four-in-one" refers to the building surrounded by four sides, forming a "mouth" shape. During the Ming and Qing Dynasties, the Forbidden City was a courtyard; of course it was very large. A courtyard building can be divided into courtyard, festoon gate, corridor, side rooms, and so on. Different rooms have their own functions. In the courtyard, the main room is situated in the north and facing the south. The foundation of the room is high, and it is the master's bedroom. The rooms on both sides are usually the residences of the children. The lower rooms are mainly for sundries, and a few also serve as kitchens. In an extended family, rooms are allocated according to seniority. The courtyard building is a closed house with strong privacy. When it is closed, the whole yard will be its own. Inside the whole courtyard, all the doors of the rooms in each side are open to the courtyard, making it very suitable for living.

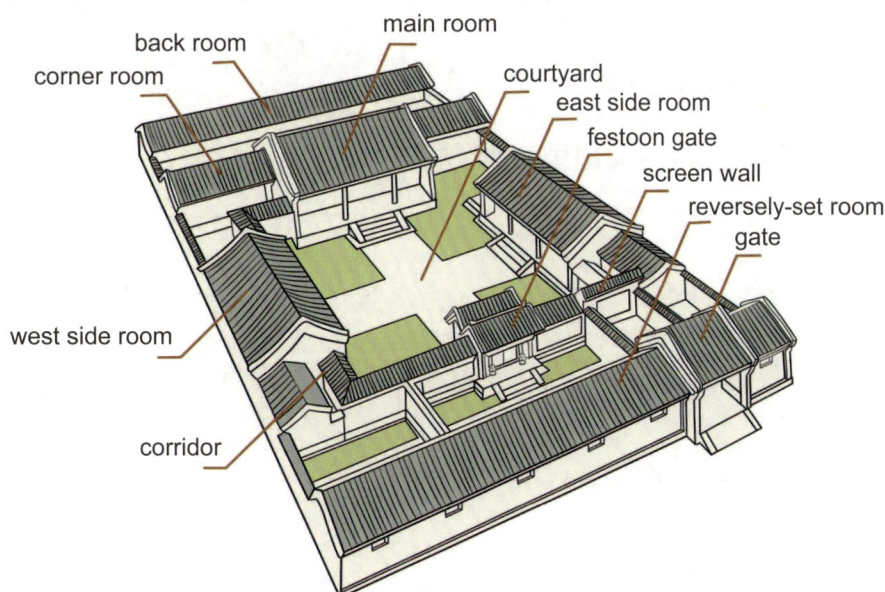

back room
main room
corner room
courtyard
east side room
festoon gate
screen wall
reversely-set room
gate
west side room
corridor

石库门与弄堂

　　上海传统的典型住宅建筑叫作石库门。石库门多集中在上海原有的租界地区，且多由开发商成片修建而成。随着城市开发，很多石库门都消失了，但是在新天地和田子坊等地还保留了不少石库门建筑。早期石库门诞生于19世纪70年代，与传统的江南民居十分相似。由于上海土地有限，人们把原来在平面铺排的江南民居变成了上下二楼的建筑。20世纪以后，由于华洋杂居、西风东渐及租界当局的要求，石库门在大规模建造中采用了北美的红松、欧洲的玻璃等，渐渐在传统中式中融入了大量的西式元素，形成了中西合璧的特点。

　　在上海的石库门中，亭子间可以说是最富原创性的建筑。亭子间产生在后期石库门里弄建筑时期，是夹在灶披间（厨房、灶间）与晒台之间的房间。亭子间原本是储物间，但随着城市人口增加，许多收入不高的市民只能选择这种租金便宜的亭子间居住。亭子间的下面是酷热难耐的

Shikumen and Longtang

The typical traditional residential buildings in Shanghai are called Shikumen buildings. Shikumen buildings are mainly concentrated in the original concession areas of Shanghai, and are mostly built in large blocks by developers. With the development of the city, many Shikumen buildings have disappeared, but some have remained in Xintiandi and Tianzifang areas in Shanghai. The early Shikumen buildings were born in the 1870s, which were very similar to the traditional folk houses in the south of the Yangtze River. Because of the limited land in Shanghai, the planar dwellings have been transformed into two-story buildings. After the 20th century, due to the influx of a large number of foreigners and Western cultures into Shanghai, coupled with the requirements of the concession authorities, North American red pine, European glass, and other foreign architectural elements are adopted in the construction of Shikumen buildings. It has gradually changed from traditional Chinese style to a combination of Chinese and Western elements, forming the characteristics of "integration of Chinese and Western styles".

In the Shikumen buildings of Shanghai, Tingzijian can be said to be the most original building. During the later period of Shikumen Lane construction, Tingzijian was sandwiched between the kitchen and the balcony. It used to be a storage room, but with the increase of urban population, many low-income citizens can only choose to live in it with low rent. Below the Tingzijian is the kitchen, which is

厨房，上面是风吹雨淋的晒台，坐南朝北，可以说是石库门里条件最差的房间。上海由于城市发展过快，居住人口迅速增长，号称在一个石库门中居住着"72家房客"，亭子间正是这种现象的典型代表。

上海的老弄堂，俗称"里弄"，是由很多一排排紧密联体而立的石库门单元组成的庞大房屋群体。"里"指的是居民聚集的地方，"弄"指的是建筑物间的夹缝通道，里弄是由相连小弄组成的住宅群。

上海的弄堂口上方总有一块标志坊。标志坊是牌坊类的一种，如泰安里，上方刻有建造年份，作为弄堂空间段落的分隔和标志之用。老里弄大多有过街楼，大部分是一层，少数二层，甚至有三层的，用作居室，楼底下腾空，供弄堂内人车通行。

extremely hot and difficult to endure. Above the Tingzijian is the flat roof exposed to wind and rain. Situated in the south of the building and facing the north, it is the worst room in the Shikumen building. Because of the rapid development of the city and the rapid growth of the residential population in Shanghai, it is said that there are 72 tenants living in a Shikumen building, and Tingzijian is the typical representative of this phenomenon.

The old Shanghai Longtang, commonly known as "Li Long", is a huge housing group consisting of many closely connected rows of Shikumen units. "Li" refers to the place where residents gather, and "Long" refers to the joint passage between buildings, which is a residential group composed of connected lanes.

There is always an iconic archway above the entrance of the Longtang (lanes) in Shanghai, which is a kind of archway, such as Tai'anli, with the construction year on it, as a mark and the separation with other lanes. Most of old lanes have overhead buildings, and most of them are single-storeyed, with a few being two-storeyed or even three-storeyed. They are used as living rooms, and the space below is for people and cars to pass in the lane hall.

中国人的购房观

有这样一个网络笑话——中国老太太说："我攒够了30年的钱，晚年终于买了一套房子。"美国老太太说："我住了30年的大房子，晚年终于还清了贷款。"虽然这只是个笑话，但也在一定程度上反映了中国人喜欢先存钱后消费的习惯。然而，在房价飞速上涨的现代社会，已经有越来越多的人选择贷款买房。对于刚参加工作的年轻人来说，租房还是买房是难以逃避的一项选择，而在中国人的传统观念里，房子不仅仅是一个建筑空间，更代表了"家"。

出于对安定感的一种心理需要，中国人十分看重房子。房子在中国人心中已经不仅是住的需要，还有资产增值的需要，甚至在某种程度上是个人实力的自我彰显。

Chinese People's Concept of Buying Houses

There goes an online joke: An old Chinese lady says, "I saved enough money for 30 years and finally bought a house in my old age." "I lived in a big house for 30 years and finally paid off my loan in my old age," an old American lady replies. Although this is only a joke, it also reflects to a certain extent that Chinese people like to save money first and then consume. However, in the modern society where house prices are soaring, more and more people have chosen to borrow money to buy houses. For young people who have just started to work, renting or buying a house is an unavoidable choice. In the traditional Chinese concept, a house is not only a building space, but also a "home".

A psychological need for a sense of stability has led Chinese people to attach great importance to houses. The house in the hearts of the Chinese people is not only a place to live in, but also the means to increase the value of assets, and even to a certain extent reflects the financial strength of an individual.

4. 重点词汇

功能

亭子间原本的**功能**是什么？

分配

住在四合院的大家庭，是根据什么来**分配**住房的？

修建

石库门一般是由谁来**修建**的？

中西合璧

除了石库门，还有哪些**中西合璧**的建筑？

5. 实践活动

（1）小组活动，参观一处典型的中国住宅（如上海的田子坊等），以报告的形式总结小组成员观察到的该处中国住宅的特征。

（2）探究中文里面把出租房子的人叫作"房东"的原因。

（3）通过上网查阅资料等方式，从多方面比较北京四合院和上海石库门建筑的不同风格。

4. Keywords

function

What is the original **function** of Tingzijian?

allocation

What is the basis of housing **allocation** for large families living in courtyard buildings?

build

Who **built** the Shikumen buildings?

integration of Chinese and Western styles

Apart from Shikumen buildings, what are other buildings that have the **integration of Chinese and Western styles**?

5. Activities

(1) In groups, visit a typical Chinese residence (such as Tianzifang in Shanghai) and summarize the characteristics of the Chinese residence observed by the group members in a report.

(2) Explore why people who rent houses to others are called "fangdong" in Chinese.

(3) Search the Internet and compare the different styles of Beijing courtyard and Shanghai Shikumen buildings from various aspects.

（4）设计一张调查表，了解中国人的住房情况，并与自己国家的情况相比较（可询问自己的父母）。

（5）在目前住房紧张的情况下，保护石库门、四合院等传统建筑是否有相应的意义和价值？为什么？

（6）在你们国家，有哪些独具特色的建筑？它们的建筑风格是什么样的？它们与四合院或石库门等相比，最大的区别是什么？与同学交流一下。

6. 自我评估

	😊	😐	☹️
（1）我了解石库门和四合院在设计上的差异。			
（2）我知道中国人为什么更愿意买房而不是租房。			
（3）我了解保护石库门等传统建筑的文化意义。			

(4) Design a questionnaire to understand the housing situation of Chinese people and compare it with that of your own country (you may ask your parents).

(5) In the current situation of housing shortage, does it have corresponding significance and value to protect Shikumen, the courtyard buildings and other traditional buildings? Why?

(6) What are the unique buildings in your country? What kinds of architectural styles do they have? What are the biggest differences between them and courtyard buildings or Shikumen? Exchange ideas with your classmates.

6. Self-assessment

	🙂	😐	☹️
(1) I understand the differences in design between Shikumen and the courtyard buildings.			
(2) I know why Chinese people prefer to buy houses rather than rent them.			
(3) I understand the cultural significance of protecting Shikumen and other traditional buildings.			

第五课　中国高铁

1. 学习目标

（1）了解高铁和其他类型火车的异同。

（2）了解中国高铁的发展。

（3）了解在12306网站上购票的方式。

2. 热身活动

讨论

（1）谁发明了铁路？与其他交通工具相比，铁路有什么优点？

（2）世界上最早的高铁是哪个国家建设的？

（3）高铁、动车和磁悬浮有什么异同？

（4）在你们国家，人们去外地常坐火车吗？为什么？

3. 阅读课文

中国的火车类型

火车票价格实惠。火车速度快，与人们的生活密切相关。其实火车也是分

Lesson Five China's High-Speed Railways

1. Learning objectives

(1) Learn the similarities and differences between high-speed railways and other types of trains.

(2) Learn the development of China's high-speed railways.

(3) Know how to buy train tickets via the website 12306.cn.

2. Warm-up

Discussion

(1) Who invented the railway? What are the advantages of railway compared with other means of transportation?

(2) Which country first built the high-speed railway in the world?

(3) What are the differences among high-speed railways, bullet trains and maglev trains?

(4) Do people often go to other places by train in your country? Why?

3. Reading texts

Classification of Trains in China

Train tickets are affordable. Trains are fast, and closely related to people's lives. In fact, trains can be divided into several types. So what kinds of trains are

种类的。那么目前中国有哪些类型的火车呢?

中国国内的火车根据速度分为不同种类。车次号一般由字母开头,代表火车的种类。例如,Z19表示直达列车,D316表示动车。

高铁是中国长途客运列车中最快的列车之一,最高时速可达350公里/时,但是在不同线路上,列车时速被限制为300公里/时到200公里/时。高铁车次号字母为G。

动车最高时速为250公里/时,车次号字母为D。动车主要运行于大城市之间快速和频繁的干线,如北京—上海、上海—苏州、深圳—广州。

直达特快列车是长途客运列车中仅次于高速列车的最好的火车,最高时速可达160公里/时。直达特快列车一般直接从出发站开到终点站,中途没有停靠站,只有个别列车有少量停靠站。车次号字母为Z。

特快列车行驶途中一般有几个停靠站,主要是大城市。特快列车的最高时速为140公里/时。大部分特快列车都设有空调,有软卧、硬卧、软座和硬座四个席别。车次号字母为T。

快车的最高时速为120公里/时,停靠站比特快列车多。快车内也设有空调,有软卧、硬卧、软座和硬座四个席别。车次号字母为K。

there in China now?

Domestic trains in China are classified according to speed. The number of trains usually starts with letters, which represent the type of trains. For example, Z19 is a direct train and D316 is a bullet train.

High-speed railway is one of the fastest long-distance passenger trains in China, with a maximum speed of 350 km/h. However, on different lines, train speed is limited to 300 km/h to 200 km/h. The letter of the high-speed railway is G.

The maximum speed of a bullet train is 250 km/h, and its train number starts with letter D. It mainly runs on fast and frequent trunk lines between big cities, such as Beijing-Shanghai, Shanghai-Suzhou, and Shenzhen-Guangzhou.

The direct express train is the best train in the long-distance passenger train after the high-speed railway, with the highest speed of 160 km/h. Direct express trains usually run directly from the departure station to the terminal station. There are no stops in the middle of the way, or only a few stops for individual trains. The train number starts with letter Z.

As for an express train, there are usually several stops on the way, mainly in big cities. The maximum speed of an express train is 140 km/h. Most express trains are equipped with air conditioners, with ticket options including soft sleeper, hard sleeper, soft seat, and hard seat. The train number begins with letter T.

The maximum speed of the fast train is 120 km/h, with more stops than the express train. There are also air conditioners in the fast trains, with ticket options including soft sleeper, hard sleeper, soft seat and hard seat. The train number begins with letter K.

普快和普客列车的车次号只有四个数字，没有字母。这两种列车是所有火车中最慢的，中途有许多停靠站。

中国高铁线路的发展

从2012到2017年，中国基本建成了世界最大的"四纵四横"高铁网。中国目前速度最快的"复兴号"动车组正以每小时350公里的速度驰骋在京沪高铁上，使中国成为世界上高铁商业运营速度最快的国家。中国高铁在实现速度跨越的同时，运营里程也从不足1万公里延展到2.2万多公里，占世界高铁运营总里程的60%多。

2016年7月，中国公布了新的《中长期铁路网规划》，明确提出在"四纵四横"高铁网的基础上规划建设"八纵八横"高铁网。目前"八纵八横"高铁网中最北边"一横"的重要组成部分——哈尔滨到牡丹江高铁最长隧道虎峰岭隧道已经顺利贯通，哈牡高铁建成后，哈尔滨到牡丹江运行时间将由目前的四个多小时缩减到一个半小时，未来还将对接京哈高铁，融入全国高铁网。

There are only four numbers and no letters in the train numbers of regular express and ordinary trains. These two trains are the slowest of all trains, with many stops on the way.

Development of China's High-Speed Railway System

From 2012 to 2017, China basically completed the world's largest "four vertical and four horizontal" high-speed railway network. China's fastest bullet train, the Fuxing, is speeding along the Beijing-Shanghai line at 350 kilometers per hour, making China rank the first in the world to run high-speed trains commercially. While the speed of railway has been improved, its operating mileage has also increased from less than 10,000 km to more than 22,000 km, accounting for more than 60% of the world's total high-speed railway mileage.

In July 2016, China released the new "Medium- and Long-term Railway Network Plan", which clearly proposed the construction of the "eight vertical and eight horizontal" high-speed railway network on the basis of the "four vertical and four horizontal" one. At present, the Hufengling Tunnel, the longest high-speed railway tunnel from Harbin to Mudanjiang, has been successfully completed, which is an important part of the "eight vertical and eight horizontal" high-speed railway network in the north. After the completion of this high-speed railway, the running time from Harbin to Mudanjiang will be reduced from the current time of more than four hours to only one and a half hours. In the future, it will connect with the high-speed railway from Beijing to Harbin and integrate into the national high-speed railway network.

"八纵八横"高铁网中，新规划的纵向线路有：呼和浩特到南宁的呼南通道；北京到昆明的京昆通道；包头到海口的包海通道；兰州到广州的兰广通道。新规划的横向线路有：绥芬河到满洲里的绥满通道；北京到兰州的京兰通道；厦门到重庆的厦渝通道；广州到昆明的广昆通道。

"八纵八横"高铁网建成后，全国高速铁路总里程将达到4.5万公里，比现在增加一倍。它将连接起总里程超过20万公里的全国铁路网，基本覆盖20万人口以上的城市。

中国为什么要发展高铁？

经过十几年的发展建设，中国高铁的运营里程已达2.5万公里，占世界的三分之二。中国为什么要大力发展高铁呢？主要有以下几个因素。

首先，高铁改善了交通条件。中国人口多，密度高，人口流动量大。高铁大大减少了人们的出行时间，提升了出行品质，同时以安全、

In the "eight vertical and eight horizontal" high-speed railway network, the new planned vertical lines include: Huhhot-Nanning Line, Beijing-Kunming Line, Baotou-Haikou Line, and Lanzhou-Guangzhou Line. The new planned horizontal routes include Suifenhe-Manchuria Line, Beijing-Lanzhou Line, Xiamen-Chongqing Line, and Guangzhou-Kunming Line.

When the "eight vertical and eight horizontal" high-speed railway network is completed, the total length of high-speed railway in China will reach 45,000 kilometers, which will double the current length. It will connect the national railway network with a total length of more than 200,000 kilometers and basically cover cities with a population of more than 200,000.

Why Should China Develop High-Speed Railways?

After more than a decade of development and construction, China has 25,000 kilometers of high-speed railways in service, more than two-thirds of the world's total. Why does China energetically develop high-speed railways? There are several factors.

Firstly, high-speed railways improve traffic conditions. As we all know, China has a large population, a high population density, and a large population flow. High-speed railways greatly reduce people's travel time, improve travel quality, and are favored by Chinese people for their safety, convenient transfer,

换乘方便、乘坐舒适等特点受到人们的青睐。

其次，高铁促进了经济发展。中国幅员辽阔，经济、资源分布不均，高铁所到之处对沿线经济起到了助推和均衡的作用，加快了城市化的进程，带动了经济欠发达地区的投资开发，促进了交通经济带的形成和高铁新城的崛起。

最后，高铁带动了制造业转型升级。高铁的投资建设带动了相关制造业的发展，有利于产业的升级和结构调整，以及产品的更新换代。高铁是一个国家制造业和科技水平的全方位展现，对提升民族荣誉感、自信心具有积极意义。

总之，中国高铁的发展可以说对很多方面都有着重要意义和深远影响。

高铁的购票方式

在中国，除了直接在火车站购票以外，还可以在12306网站购票。在12306网站上，人们可以看到车次和价格，提前20天就可以购票。这样的购票方式既安全又便捷。如果你出去旅游或探亲访友，不妨试试。

and comfortable ride.

Secondly, high-speed railways promote the country's economic development. With a vast territory and uneven distribution of economic resources, China's high-speed railways play a role in promoting and balancing the economy along the route, accelerating the urbanization process, driving the investment and development in underdeveloped areas, promoting the formation of transportation economic belt and the rise of new high-speed railway cities.

Thirdly, high-speed railways transform and upgrade the manufacturing industry. They drive the development of related industry, which is conducive to industrial upgrading and structural adjustment, and product upgrading. Thus, high-speed railways are the all-around display of a country's manufacturing and technological capabilities, which is of positive significance to enhance the sense of national honor and self-confidence.

All in all, there is a lot of important significance and far-reaching impact on many aspects with the development of China's high-speed railways.

High-Speed Rail Ticketing Method

In China, in addition to purchasing tickets directly at the train station, people can also buy tickets on the website 12306.cn. They can visit the website and find the train numbers and prices. The tickets can be purchased 20 days in advance. This way of purchasing tickets is safe and convenient. If you are going out for a trip or visiting friends and relatives, just try it.

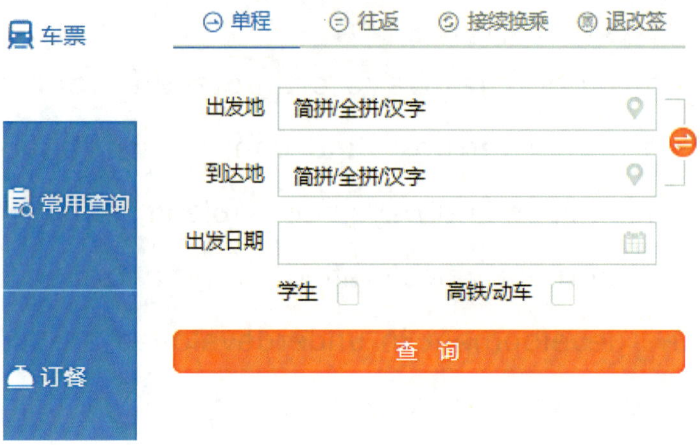

| 🚈 车票 | ⊖ 单程　　⊟ 往返　　⊙ 接续换乘　　⊗ 退改签 |

🔍 常用查询	出发地　简拼/全拼/汉字
	到达地　简拼/全拼/汉字
🛎 订餐	出发日期
	学生 ☐　　高铁/动车 ☐
	查 询

　　在繁忙的铁路运输线路上，每天都有成百上千的高铁、动车在风驰电掣地运行。它们将中国的各个地方连结起来，漫长的时间与遥远的路程从此不再成为人们团聚的阻碍。

4. 重点词汇

铁路

世界上最早的**铁路**在哪里？

高铁

哪个国家最早建设**高铁**？

动车

动车和高铁有什么区别？

特快

特快火车的车次号字母是什么？

车票 | ⊙ 单程 | ⊖ 往返 | ⊙ 接续换乘 | ⊛ 退改签

出发地　简拼/全拼/汉字　⚲

到达地　简拼/全拼/汉字　⚲

出发日期　📅

学生 ☐　　高铁/动车 ☐

查　询

常用查询

订餐

On the busy railway lines, hundreds of high-speed railways and bullet trains run at galloping speeds every day. They connect the different places in China, and the long journey is no longer an obstacle to people's reunion.

4. Keywords

railway

Where is the earliest **railway** in the world?

high-speed railway

Which country built the first **high-speed railway**?

bullet train

What are the differences between **bullet trains** and high-speed railways?

express train

What is the letter in the train numbers for the **express train**?

火车票

如果要网络购买**火车票**，可以去哪个网站？

5. 实践活动

（1）看一看下面的火车票，告诉同学上面包含哪些信息。

（2）查阅一些资料，与同学讨论一下，分析中国高铁发展如此之快的原因。

（3）高铁的发展给中国带来什么影响？给世界呢？

（4）中国高铁建设其实经历了非常艰苦的探索，请上网查资料或者阅读《高铁风云录》（湖南文艺出版社2015年版），向同学介绍一下中国高铁建设中遇到的困难。

train ticket

If you want to buy **train tickets** online, which website can you visit?

5. Activities

(1) Look at the following train ticket and tell your classmates what information it contains.

Z0000000
北京南　　G109次　　上海虹桥
BeiJingNan　　　　ShangHaiHongQiao
2019年8月8日08：15开　　06车06A号
553.00元　　网　　二等座
限乘当日当次车
王某某
123**************
123456789123456789　　北京南售

(2) Look up some information and discuss with your classmates why China's high-speed railways develop so quickly.

(3) What impact does the development of high-speed railways have on China? What about the world?

(4) The construction of China's high-speed railways has actually undergone a very arduous exploration. Please search for information on the Internet or read the book *High-Speed Rail in Colour* (Published by Hunan Literature and Art Publishing House in 2015) and introduce to your classmates the difficulties encountered in the construction of China's high-speed railways.

（5）看一看中国的高铁线路图，分析一下中国高铁线路的特点及其形成原因。

6. 自我评估

	😊	😐	😞
（1）我了解中国高铁与其他火车的差异。			
（2）我了解中国高铁的发展情况。			
（3）我会通过12306网站购票。			

(5) Look at the high-speed railway line in China, then analyze its characteristics and the reasons for its formation.

6. Self-assessment

	😊	😐	☹️
(1) I know the differences between China's high-speed railways and other trains.			
(2) I know the development of China's high-speed railway system.			
(3) I can buy train tickets via the website 12306.cn.			

第六课　中国音乐人

1. 学习目标

（1）能介绍马友友、谭盾和郎朗的生平经历。

（2）能说明古典音乐和现代音乐的不同特点。

（3）能分析马友友、谭盾和郎朗的音乐作品的特点。

2. 热身活动

讨论

（1）你知道哪些著名的音乐家？知不知道中国的音乐家？

（2）你认为一位成功的音乐家需要具备哪些素质？天赋、努力和机遇，哪一个最重要？你认为音乐家应该多学习其他学科的知识吗？

（3）你喜欢流行音乐还是古典音乐？为什么？你觉得为什么古典音乐能受到很多人的喜爱？

（4）你会表演什么乐器？你是怎么学的？

Lesson Six   Chinese Musicians

1. Learning objectives

(1) Be able to introduce the life experiences of Yo-Yo Ma, Tan Dun, and Lang Lang.

(2) Be able to explain the different characteristics of classical and modern music.

(3) Be able to analyze the characteristics of the works of Yo-Yo Ma, Tan Dun, and Lang Lang.

2. Warm-up

Discussion

(1) Do you know any famous musicians? Do you know Chinese musicians?

(2) What qualities do you think a successful musician needs? Among talent, effort, and opportunity, which is the most important? Do you think musicians should learn more about other subjects?

(3) Do you like pop music or classical music? Why? Why do you think classical music can be loved by many people?

(4) What instrument can you play? How did you learn it?

马友友

1955年10月7日，马友友出生在法国巴黎。他的父亲是中国有名的音乐教育家和小提琴演奏家马孝俊。马友友4岁开始学习大提琴，不久他随家人定居纽约。7岁那年，他参加了为筹建华盛顿文化中心举行的巡回义演音乐会，他和姐姐一同登台表演，当时坐在台下观看这场演出的还有肯尼迪总统夫妇。1971年，16岁的马友友在纽约卡内基音乐厅举行独奏音乐会。高中毕业后，他没有选择专门的音乐学院，而是去了哈佛大学学习人类学和考古学。2006年，时任联合国秘书长安南任命马友友为联合国和平使者。2011年，时任美国总统奥巴马为马友友等人颁发了总统自由勋章。

在马友友看来，父亲是他一生中最重要的启蒙老师。在一次采访中，他说："我的父亲是一位非常棒的老师，我从来没有花费大量的时间练习，他教会我怎么高效率地学习和思考。"对于演奏，他有着自己独特的思考。他说："我不考虑在什么地方演奏，也不考虑在哪里，我只考虑我的观众是谁，我该怎么演奏。"

谭 盾

1957年，谭盾出生于湖南，他从小就受到了当地文化的影响。谭盾的青年时代是在农村度过的。后来，他考上了中央音乐学院，学习指挥和作曲专业。硕士毕业后，他如愿以偿地来到哥伦比亚大学攻读博士学位。留学美国期间，他成了著名音乐人小泽征尔的学生，逐渐在国际上展露才华。1983年，谭盾创

3. Reading texts

Yo-Yo Ma

Yo-Yo Ma was born in Paris, France, on October 7, 1955. His father is Ma Xiaojun, a famous music educator and violinist in China. Yo-Yo Ma began to learn cello at the age of four, and soon settled in New York with his family. At the age of seven, he attended a concert tour aimed to raise funds for the Washington Cultural Center. He performed with his sister on stage, while President and Mrs. Kennedy were sitting in the audience watching the performance. In 1971, Yo-Yo Ma, at the age of 16, gave a solo concert at Carnegie Hall in New York. After graduating from high school, instead of choosing a music college, he went to Harvard University to study anthropology and archaeology. In 2006, the then UN Secretary-General Annan appointed Yo-Yo Ma as the UN Peace Envoy. In 2011, the then President Barack Obama awarded Yo-Yo Ma and others the Presidential Medal of Freedom.

In Yo-Yo Ma's opinion, his father is the most important teacher in his life. In an interview, he said, "My father is a very good teacher. I never spent a lot of time practicing. He taught me how to study and think efficiently." For playing, he has his own unique thinking. He said, "I don't think about where to play. I just think about who my audience is and how I should play."

Tan Dun

Tan Dun was born in Hunan in 1957 and was influenced by local culture. Tan Dun spent his youth in the countryside. Later, he enrolled in Central Conservatory of Music, majoring in conducting and composing. After getting his master's degree, he came to Columbia University to pursue his doctorate. During his study

作的《风雅颂》赢得了国际作曲大奖。后来他又接连获得了多个大奖，其中有第71届奥斯卡最佳原创音乐奖、格莱美作曲大奖和德国巴赫奖。

谭盾的成功与他的勤奋是分不开的。他不仅对音乐感兴趣，也坚持写作。他每天都会花6个小时的时间写作。谭盾的作品既有楚汉文化的特点，也有现代音乐的创新。他崇尚"文化兼容"，喜欢多种风格、多种文化的结合。

不仅如此，谭盾也是一位想象力非常丰富的作曲家，生活中的任何声音对他来说都可以变成音乐。谭盾在创作《神秘的土地：12把大提琴和乐队的协奏曲》时，让演奏者尽情演绎自己的故事，每一位演奏者每一次的演奏都不一样。这样的做法在演奏形式上有了极大的创新，也给演奏者带来了挑战。

郎　朗

作为中国的"80后"，郎朗已经跻身于世界最优秀的钢琴家行列。但是郎朗的成才之路并不是一帆风顺的。郎朗出生在中国辽宁的一个普通家庭。小时候的郎朗喜欢看动画片《猫和老鼠》，其中弹钢琴的画面让郎朗喜欢上了钢琴。于是父母决定让郎朗学习钢琴。

in the United States, he became a student of the famous musician Seiji Ozawa and gradually showed his talent in the international arena. In 1983, Tan Dun's *Ode to Elegance* won the International Composition Award. Later, he won several awards, including the 71st Academy Award for Best Original Music, the Grammy Award for Composition and the German Bach Award.

Tan Dun's success is inseparable from his diligence. He is not only interested in music, but also passionate about writing. He spends six hours writing every day. Tan Dun's works not only have the characteristics of Chu and Han cultures, but also have the innovations of modern music. He advocates "cultural compatibility" and likes the combination of various styles and cultures.

Tan Dun is an imaginative composer and any sound in life can become music for him. While creating *Mysterious Land—12 Cellos and Orchestra Concertos*, Tan Dun let the performers fully demonstrate their own stories, with each performer performing differently each time. This practice has made great innovations in the form of performance, and also brought challenges to the performers.

Lang Lang

Born in the 1980s, Lang Lang has become one of the best pianists in the world. However, Lang Lang's road to success was not smooth. Lang Lang was born in an ordinary family in Liaoning Province, China. As a child, Lang Lang liked to watch the cartoon *Tom and Jerry*. The picture of playing the piano in the cartoon made Lang Lang like the piano. So his parents decided to let Lang Lang learn the piano.

儿时的郎朗练琴非常刻苦。父亲对他也非常严格，经过了几年的苦练，郎朗的进步非常迅速。1991年，郎朗的父母做了一个艰难的决定：父亲辞去工作，带郎朗去北京求学。9岁的郎朗来到中央音乐学院学习钢琴。但是老师觉得郎朗没有音乐天赋，劝他离开。在经历了各种打击和痛苦之后，他们父子俩盼来了希望。著名音乐教育家赵屏国教授愿意教授郎朗。郎朗后来回忆道："我几乎要放弃一切了，但之后我决定要向所有人展示我的才华。"

事实上，郎朗真的做到了！1993年，11岁的他在德国"第四届世界青少年钢琴大赛"上获得了冠军。后来他留学美国，在美国柯蒂斯音乐学院学习。机会总是留给有准备的人。1999年，在芝加哥拉维尼亚音乐节明星演奏会中，郎朗替代生病的钢琴演奏家安德烈·瓦兹演奏，一举成名。人们不仅喜欢他精彩的音乐演奏，还被他丰富的肢体语言打动。视觉和听觉上的双重盛宴让郎朗在国际上享有盛名。

4. 重点词汇

作品

贝多芬最著名的**作品**是什么？

When he was a child, Lang Lang practiced the piano very hard. His father was very strict with him. After years of hard training, Lang Lang made rapid progress. In 1991, Lang Lang's parents made a difficult decision: His father quit his job and took him to Beijing to study. Lang Lang, at the age of nine, came to the Central Conservatory of Music to study piano. Unfortunately, the teacher thought Lang Lang had no musical talent and advised him to leave. After all kinds of blows and pains, Lang Lang and his father saw hope. Professor Zhao Pingguo, a famous music educator, was willing to teach Lang Lang. Lang Lang later recalled, "I almost gave up everything, but then I decided to show everyone my talent."

In fact, Lang Lang really did it! In 1993, at the age of 11, he won the 4th World Youth Piano Competition in Germany. Later, he went to the United States and studied at Curtis Conservatory of Music. Opportunities come to those who are prepared. In 1999, Lang Lang became famous as a replacement for the sick pianist Andre Watts in the celebrity concert at Chicago Lavinia Music Festival. People not only like his wonderful music performance, but also are moved by his rich body language. The musical feast for both eyes and ears makes Lang Lang famous in the world.

4. Keywords

works

What are Beethoven's most famous **works**?

作曲家

中国著名的**作曲家**有谁？

大提琴

大提琴和小提琴有什么不一样？

钢琴

怎么样可以弹好**钢琴**？

演奏

婚礼上适合**演奏**什么乐曲？生日会上呢？

5. 实践活动

（1）马友友演奏的专辑《生命之歌》共收录了19首大提琴与钢琴合作的乐曲，涉及宗教、母爱、青年叛逆、爱情以及死亡等主题。请欣赏专辑《生命之歌》，选择一个你最喜爱的作品，并说明你喜爱它的理由。

（2）贝多芬是西方著名的作曲家，谭盾是中国著名的作曲家。请欣赏贝多芬作曲的《命运交响曲》和谭盾作曲的《风雅颂》。讨论一下为什么有人说"贝多芬与谭盾这两位作曲家都对音乐进行了大胆的创新"。

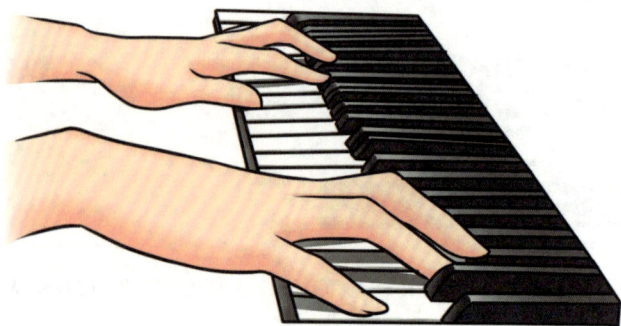

composer

Who are the famous Chinese **composers**?

cello

What is the difference between **cello** and violin?

piano

How can you play the **piano** well?

play

What music is suitable to **play** at a wedding or at a birthday party?

5. Activities

(1) Yo-Yo Ma's album *Songs from the Arc of Life* contains 19 cello and piano duets, covering such themes as religion, maternal love, youth rebellion, love, and death. Please enjoy the album, choose one of your favorite works, and explain why you like it.

(2) Beethoven is a famous Western composer. Tan Dun is a famous Chinese composer. Please enjoy Beethoven's *Symphony of Destiny* and Tan Dun's *Ode to Elegance.* Discuss why some people say that both Beethoven and Tan Dun have made bold innovations in music.

（3）第73届奥斯卡最佳外语片《卧虎藏龙》的主题曲是谭盾作曲的，演奏者是马友友。请观看电影《卧虎藏龙》并欣赏主题曲《卧虎藏龙》，结合电影，谈谈你喜欢主题曲的哪一部分，以及不喜欢哪一部分。

（4）请欣赏郎朗弹奏的《保卫黄河》和中国交响乐团合唱团演唱的《保卫黄河》，谈谈你的体会。

保卫黄河（节选）

词：光未然

曲：冼星海

风在吼/马在叫/黄河在咆哮/黄河在咆哮

河西山冈万丈高/河东河北高粱熟了

万山丛中/抗日英雄真不少/青纱帐里/游击健儿逞英豪

端起了土枪洋枪/挥动着大刀长矛

保卫家乡/保卫黄河/保卫华北/保卫全中国

(3) The theme song of the 73rd Academy Award for Best Foreign Language Film *Crouching Tiger, Hidden Dragon* was composed by Tan Dun and played by Yo-Yo Ma. Please watch the movie and enjoy the theme song. Taking the movie into consideration, which part of the theme song do you like? Which part do you dislike?

(4) Please enjoy *Defending the Yellow River* played by Lang Lang and sung by the China National Symphony Orchestra Chorus. Talk about your feelings after enjoying it.

Defending the Yellow River (An Excerpt)

Lyricist: Guang Weiran

Composer: Xian Xinghai

The wind is roaring / the horse is shouting / the Yellow River is roaring / the Yellow River is roaring

To the west of the river, there are many high mountains / to the east and the north the sorghum is ripe

In the mountains / Anti-Japanese heroes really many / In the green and thick crops / Guerrilla fighters are waiting to fight

Pick up the gun / wave the spear and knife

Defending home / Defending the Yellow River / Defending North China/ Defending the whole motherland

（5）马友友的专辑《歌咏乡愁》（共13章）由丝绸之路沿线上不同民族的民谣组成。请欣赏这张专辑并找出你最喜欢的曲目，然后试着向同学介绍这首曲目的音乐特点。

6. 自我评估

	🙂	😐	☹️
（1）我能说出马友友、谭盾和郎朗的经历。			
（2）我能说明马友友、谭盾和郎朗的作品特点。			
（3）我能分析古典音乐和现代音乐的特点。			

(5) Yo-Yo Ma's album *Sing Me Home* (all together 13 chapters) is composed of ballads of different nationalities along the Silk Road. Please enjoy this album and find out your favorite tune, then try to introduce its music characteristics.

6. Self-assessment

	🙂	😐	🙁
(1) I can tell the experiences of Yo-Yo Ma, Tan Dun, and Lang Lang.			
(2) I can explain the characteristics of the works of Yo-Yo Ma, Tan Dun, and Lang Lang.			
(3) I can analyze the characteristics of classical music and modern music.			

第七课 丝绸之路和"一带一路"

1. 学习目标

（1）能说明"一带一路"的含义。

（2）能向他人介绍古丝绸之路的历史及其对世界的影响。

（3）能说明张骞通西域和郑和下西洋的历史。

2. 热身活动

讨论

（1）你听过"丝绸之路"这个名词吗？它是谁提出来的？为什么叫"丝绸之路"？

（2）丝绸之路途经哪些国家？请在地图上指出来。

（3）看地图后，跟同学讨论一下：古代有哪些路线可以从中国到欧洲？

（4）你听过"一带一路"这个名词吗？它的含义是什么？

Lesson Seven   The Silk Road and the Belt and Road Initiative

1. Learning objectives

(1) Be able to explain the meaning of the Belt and Road Initiative.

(2) Be able to introduce to others the history of the ancient Silk Road and its impact on the world.

(3) Be able to explain the history of Zhang Qian's mission to the Western Regions and Zheng He's voyages to the Western Seas.

2. Warm-up

Discussion

(1) Have you heard the term "Silk Road"? Do you know who put it forward? Why is it called the Silk Road?

(2) What are the countries along the Silk Road? Please point them out on the map.

(3) After reading the map, discuss with your classmates what ancient routes could be taken from China to Europe.

(4) Have you heard the term "the Belt and Road Initiative"? What does it mean?

3. 阅读课文

张骞通西域

从前，在蒙古草原上，有一个非常强悍的部落，叫匈奴。它曾是汉朝最强大的对手。汉武帝很想联合另一个部落大月氏来抗击匈奴，于是派张骞出使西域。公元前138年，张骞带着100多人从长安出发前往西域。途中他被匈奴人抓到，扣押多年之后成功脱逃，继续向西寻找大月氏。后来张骞来到了大宛国，向大宛国王说明了自己的目的，并请求国王能够派人帮助他们完成使命。大宛国王很快被张骞说服了，于是想办法把他们送到了大月氏。没想到的是，由于大月氏人觉得新的国土十分肥沃，并且离匈奴很远，已经放弃了抗击匈奴的想法。张骞没有说服大月氏的国王，不得不离开了大月氏，回到了长安。虽然这次出使没有达到联合西域大月氏的目的，但是张骞向皇帝详细地报告了自己的经历和见闻，使汉朝对西域各国的地理、经济和文化都有了比较详细的了解。

公元122年，张骞带着4支探险队又一次出使西域。这一次他们分开行动，带着很多贵重的礼品出使各个国家。这次出使比较顺利，使更多的国家了解到

3. Reading texts

Zhang Qian's Mission to the Western Regions

Once upon a time, on the Mongolian grassland, there was a very strong tribe called Hun. It was the most powerful rival of the Han Dynasty. Emperor Wudi of the Han Dynasty wanted to unite another tribe, Dayuezhi, to fight the Huns, so he sent Zhang Qian to the Western Regions. In 138 B.C., Zhang Qian took more than 100 people from Chang'an to the Western Regions. On the way, he was caught by the Huns. After many years of detention, he succeeded in escaping and continued to search for Dayuezhi to the west. Later, Zhang Qian came to Dawan and explained his purpose to the King of Dawan. He asked the King to send someone to help them accomplish their mission. The King of Dawan was soon convinced by Zhang Qian, so he managed to send them to Dayuezhi. Unexpectedly, because the Dayue people thought the new land was very fertile and far away from the Huns, they had abandoned the idea of fighting against the Huns. Zhang Qian did not persuade the King of Dayuezhi, so he had to leave Dayuezhi and return to Chang'an. Although Zhang Qian did not achieve the goal of uniting Dayuezhi in the Western Regions, he reported his experiences to the emperor in detail, which made the Han Dynasty have a more detailed understanding of the geography, economy and culture of the countries in the Western Regions.

In A.D. 122, Zhang Qian again led four expedition groups to the Western Regions. This time they carried out the mission separately and traveled to various countries with many valuable gifts. The mission went smoothly, enabling more countries to understand the prosperity of the Han Dynasty and be willing to deal with the Han Dynasty. This mission improved the relationship between the countries of the Western Regions and the Han Dynasty, and promoted the

了汉朝的富足，愿意和汉朝来往。这次出使沟通了西域各国和汉朝的联系，促进了东西方经济文化的交流，从此打通了丝绸之路。

郑和下西洋

　　郑和（1371-1433）是中国历史上伟大的航海家。他不仅对航海十分感兴趣，也很有外交才能。1405年，明朝的皇帝决定派郑和下西洋。当时的西洋，指的是中国南海以西的地方。七月的一天，郑和带着庞大的船队从太仓刘家港出发，开始了一次中国历史上伟大的航海之旅。由于郑和运用了中国发明的指南针和其他航海技术，他们的船没有被大风大浪打翻，也没有在海上迷失方向。

economic and cultural exchanges between the East and the West. From then on, the Silk Road was opened up.

Zheng He's Voyages to the Western Seas

Zheng He (1371–1433) was a great navigator in Chinese history. Not only was he interested in navigation, but he also had diplomatic talent. In 1405, the emperor of the Ming Dynasty decided to send Zheng He to the Western Seas. The Western Seas at that time refers to the area west of the South China Sea. One day in July, Zheng He set out from Liujiagang, Taicang, with a huge fleet, on a great voyage in Chinese history. Because Zheng He used the compass and other navigational techniques invented by China, their ship was not overturned by strong winds and waves, nor was it lost at sea. Zheng He visited Java, Old Port, Sumatra, Ceylon and other places. At every place, Zheng He visited the local kings or leaders on behalf of the emperor and presented them with valuable

郑和的这次航行访问了爪洼、旧港、苏门答腊、锡兰、故里等地。每到一个地方，郑和就代表皇帝拜访当地的国王或首领，向他们赠送贵重的礼品，还用带来的丝绸、瓷器等中国特产交换当地特产。

1407年9月，郑和等人回到北京，向皇帝讲述了一路上的经历。皇帝听了很高兴，大力支持郑和再一次下西洋。从1405年到1433年的28年间，郑和共七次远航西太平洋和印度洋，每次出行率领2万多人，拜访了30多个国家和地区，最远到达东非和红海（郑和航海线路图参见附录一）。

郑和每到一地，都受到当地人民的热烈欢迎和友好接待。他每次结束访问时，都有许多外国使团（其中有国王和王族）随同来到中国。他不仅带回了各国人民的友好情谊，也带回了许多当地的特产和珍禽异兽，比如胡椒、象牙以及狮子、长颈鹿等。郑和下西洋，打开了友谊的大门。

gifts. He also exchanged the silk and porcelain he brought with him for the local specialties.

In September 1407, Zheng He and others returned to Beijing and told the emperor about their experiences along the way. The emperor was very happy to hear that and strongly supported Zheng He to go to the Western Seas again. During the 28 years from 1405 to 1433, Zheng He voyaged seven times to the Western Pacific and Indian Oceans, each time leading more than 20,000 people, visiting more than 30 countries and regions, reaching as far as East Africa and the Red Sea (see Appendix One for Zheng He's navigation route).

Everywhere Zheng He went, he was warmly welcomed and well received. Every time he finished his visit, many foreign missions, including kings and royal families, accompanied him to China. He brought back not only the friendship of the people of all countries, but also many local specialties and exotic animals, such as pepper, ivory, lions, and giraffes. Zheng He's voyages opened the door of friendship.

丝 绸 之 路

丝绸之路始于古代中国长安，是一条连接亚洲、非洲和欧洲的古代陆上商业贸易路线，最初的作用是运输古代中国出产的丝绸、瓷器等商品，后来成为东方与西方之间在经济、政治、文化等诸多方面进行交流的主要道路。张骞通西域之后使得丝绸之路变得畅通，增强了中国与西方的联系，给人们的生活带来了很多变化。

丝绸之路开通以后，有很多来自西域、中亚和西亚地区的商人来到长安城。他们为了做生意学习汉语，了解中国文化。这些商人不仅把自己国家的特产、良马、乐器和珍宝带到了中国，又把丝绸、瓷器等中国特产带回了西方。

大批外国人的到来，为长安城带来了浓郁的外国风情。生活在长安，你可以看到古罗马的浴池和拜占庭的凉亭，可以牵着乖巧的哈巴狗散步，也可以喝到香甜的葡萄酒，吃着石榴、核桃，穿着外国的服装打马球。

"一 带 一 路"

2013年9月7日，中国国家主席习近平在哈萨克斯坦纳扎尔巴耶夫大学发表题为"弘扬人民友谊 共创美好未来"的演讲，提出共同建设"丝绸之路经济带"。

The Silk Road

The Silk Road, which began in Chang'an, ancient China, was an ancient land trade route connecting Asia, Africa, and Europe. Its initial role was to transport silk, porcelain and other commodities produced in ancient China. Later, it became the main road for economic, political and cultural exchanges between the East and the West. Zhang Qian's mission to the Western Regions made the Silk Road unblocked, strengthened China's ties with the West, and brought many changes to people's lives.

After the opening up of the Silk Road, many businessmen from Western Regions, Central and Western Asia came to Chang'an. They learned Chinese and got to know Chinese culture for business. These businessmen not only brought their countries' specialties, good horses, musical instruments, and treasures to China, but also brought Chinese specialties such as silk and porcelain back to the West.

The arrival of a large number of foreigners has brought a strong exotic flavor to Chang'an. Living in Chang'an, you could see the ancient Roman baths and the Byzantine pavilions, walk cute puppies, and also drink sweet wine, eat pomegranates, walnuts, and wear foreign clothes to play polo.

The Belt and Road Initiative

On September 7, 2013, Chinese President Xi Jinping delivered a speech entitled "Promote Friendship Between Our People and Work Together to Build a Better Future" at Nazarbayev University in Kazakhstan, proposing to jointly build the "Silk Road Economic Belt".

2013年10月3日，习近平主席在印度尼西亚国会发表题为"携手建设中国—东盟命运共同体"的演讲，提出共同建设"21世纪海上丝绸之路"。

"一带一路"就是"丝绸之路经济带"和"21世纪海上丝绸之路"的简称。"一带一路"不是古丝绸之路的简单升级，而是借用古丝绸之路的历史符号，融入了新的时代内涵；"一带一路"更不是"带"和"路"的地理概念，而是中国向世界提供的国际合作平台和公共产品，是一项开放包容的经济合作倡议。

共建"一带一路"一共有五大走向，其中丝绸之路经济带有三大走向：一是从中国西北、东北经中亚、俄罗斯至欧洲、波罗的海；二是从中国西北经中亚、西亚至波斯湾、地中海；三是从中国西南经中南半岛至印度洋。21世纪海上丝绸之路有两大走向：一是从中国沿海港口过南海，经马六甲海峡到印度洋，延伸至欧洲；二是从中国沿海港口过南海，向南太平洋延伸（"一带一路"经济走廊参见附录二）。

On October 3, 2013, President Xi Jinping delivered a speech entitled "Joining Hands in Building a China-ASEAN Community of Common Destiny" at the Indonesian parliament, proposing to jointly build the "21st Century Maritime Silk Road".

The Belt and Road Initiative is the abbreviation of the "Silk Road Economic Belt" and the "21st Century Maritime Silk Road". It is not a simple upgrade of the ancient Silk Road. Instead, it takes the historical symbols of the ancient Silk Road into the new era connotation. Also, it is not the geographical concept of "belt" and "road". It is an international cooperation platform and public product provided by China to the world. It is an open and inclusive economic cooperation initiative.

There are five directions for building the Belt and Road Initiative. The Silk Road Economic Belt has three main trends: The first is from Northwest China, Northeast China via Central Asia, Russia to Europe and the Baltic Sea; the second is from Northwest China via Central Asia, West Asia to the Persian Gulf and the Mediterranean Sea; and the third is from Southwest China via the Indochina Peninsula to the Indian Ocean. The 21st Century Maritime Silk Road has two main trends: one is to cross the South China Sea from China's coastal ports, to extend to Europe from the Strait of Malacca to the Indian Ocean, and the other is to cross the South China Sea from China's coastal ports to the South Pacific (see Appendix Two for the Economic Corridor of the Belt and Road Initiative).

4. 重点词汇

丝绸之路

丝绸之路连接了哪几个大洲？

出使

张骞**出使**西域的目的是什么？

特产

你的家乡有哪些**特产**？

"一带一路"

"一带一路"是由谁提出来的？

5. 实践活动

（1）"丝绸之路"这个词最早是由德国人费迪南·冯·李希霍芬提出来的，请查阅相关资料，向同学介绍一下他。

（2）请看右边的图片，这是古代西方雕塑中身穿丝绸的雅典娜女神，想一想这张图片说明了什么。

4. Keywords

Silk Road

Which continents does the **Silk Road** connect?

mission

What is the purpose of Zhang Qian's **mission** to the Western Regions?

specialty

What **specialties** do you have in your hometown?

the Belt and Road Initiative

Who put forward the concept of **the Belt and Road Initiative**?

5. Activities

(1) "Silk Road" was first put forward by Ferdinand von Richthofen, a German. Please consult relevant materials and introduce him to your classmates.

(2) Look at the picture on the right. This is an ancient Western sculpture of Athena wearing silk. Think about what this picture shows.

（3）请看下面的两张图片，左图是2016年马六甲为了纪念郑和下西洋611周年，在最热闹的鸡场街制作了这样一幅宣传板。右图是在马来西亚发现的一个器具，下半部分是中国的青花瓷。为什么马来西亚人要纪念郑和下西洋？郑和下西洋对马来西亚和东南亚的华人华侨社会有什么影响？

（4）上网检索或者到图书馆查找资料，看看有哪些产品是通过丝绸之路从西方传到东方的，又有哪些产品是通过丝绸之路从东方传到西方的。

(3) Look at the two pictures below. The one on the left is a billboard made in 2016 on the busiest Jonker Street in Malacca to commemorate the 611th anniversary of Zheng He's voyages. The one on the right is an instrument found in Malaysia. Its bottom half is Chinese blue and white porcelain. Why do Malaysians commemorate Zheng He's voyages? What impact did Zheng He's voyages have on the overseas Chinese community in Malaysia and Southeast Asia?

(4) Search the Internet or go to the library to find information. Which things were transferred from the West to the East through the Silk Road? Which things were transferred from the East to the West through the Silk Road?

（5）尽管中国历史书上记载了郑和下西洋，但是还有人认为郑和下西洋是虚构的，他们质疑的理由主要是"当时中国根本就造不出来这么庞大的船体，而且木质结构的船只也不能进行跨洋远航"。请查阅资料，分析这种说法存在的问题。

（6）请以小组为单位，上网搜集近几年有关"一带一路"的新闻，讨论"一带一路"对中国和世界的影响。

6. 自我评估

	😊	😐	😞
（1）我能讲述张骞通西域和郑和下西洋的故事。			
（2）我能说明古代丝绸之路的历史影响。			
（3）我能说出"一带一路"的含义。			

(5) Although Zheng He's voyages were recorded in Chinese history books, some people still believe that Zheng He's voyages were fictitious. The main reason why they question it is that "at that time, China could not build such a huge hull, and wooden vessels could not make long voyages across the ocean". Please look for information and analyze the problems of this statement.

(6) In groups, collect the news about the Belt and Road Initiative in recent years, and discuss its impact on China and the world.

6. Self-assessment

	😊	😐	😠
(1) I can tell the story of Zhang Qian's mission to the Western Regions and Zheng He's voyages to the Western Seas.			
(2) I can explain the historical influence of the ancient Silk Road.			
(3) I can tell others the meaning of the Belt and Road Initiative.			

第八课 《三国演义》

1. 学习目标

（1）能说出《三国演义》的主要情节。

（2）能说明《三国演义》中主要人物的特点。

（3）能说一个《三国演义》中的经典故事。

2. 热身活动

讨论

（1）你听说过中国古代"三国"的故事吗？"三国"有什么著名人物？

（2）你们国家有没有发生过战争？在战争中有没有涌现出什么英雄人物？

（3）你觉得为什么会发生战争？如何才能避免战争的发生？

3. 阅读课文

《三国演义》简介

《三国演义》是一部中国古代长篇历史小说，是中国四大名著之一，作者是明朝的罗贯中。他根据历史上发生的事情，整理了相关的历史文献和民间故事，

Lesson Eight *Romance of the Three Kingdoms*

1. Learning objectives

(1) Be able to discuss the main plot of *Romance of the Three Kingdoms*.

(2) Be able to tell the characteristics of the main characters in *Romance of the Three Kingdoms*.

(3) Be able to tell a classic story from *Romance of the Three Kingdoms*.

2. Warm-up

Discussion

(1) Have you heard the story of the Three Kingdoms in ancient China? What are the famous figures in the Three Kingdoms?

(2) Has there been any war in your country? Did any heroes emerge in the war?

(3) Why do you think wars happened? How can wars be avoided?

3. Reading texts

Introduction to *Romance of the Three Kingdoms*

Romance of the Three Kingdoms is a long historical novel, and one of the four great classic works in China. The author is Luo Guanzhong from the Ming Dynasty. According to the historical events, Luo collected the relevant historical

125

进行了一定的艺术加工，创作了这部历史小说。

《三国演义》叙述的是从东汉末年到西晋初年之间近一百年的历史风云，全书描写了魏、蜀、吴三国之间的复杂斗争。小说反映了当时的社会矛盾和社会斗争，塑造了一批英雄人物，主要有曹操、刘备、孙权、诸葛亮、周瑜等。在对三国历史的把握上，作者表现出明显的个人倾向，他赞赏刘备的仁爱贤德，批判曹操的奸诈阴险。

《三国演义》在中国家喻户晓，其中的很多故事都为人熟知，并被传入日本、朝鲜、韩国、越南、泰国、俄罗斯等国家。

三 顾 茅 庐

在一次大战后，曹操打败了刘备。刘备非常需要有智慧的人才。刘备的手下徐庶告诉刘备，南阳有个非常聪明的人叫诸葛亮，如果能得到他的帮助，就可以得到天下了。

第二天，刘备就和关羽、张飞带着礼物，去南阳拜访诸葛亮。他们走了很远的路，终于来到了一间草屋。刘备亲自下马去敲门，一个男孩开了门，告诉刘备诸葛亮已经外出了。刘备三人只好回去。过了几天，刘备和关羽、张飞又来拜访诸葛亮。那天天气寒冷，下着大雪。刘备走到门口，听见读书声，以为

documents and folk stories, carried out certain artistic processing, and created this historical novel.

Romance of the Three Kingdoms describes nearly a hundred years of history from the end of the Eastern Han Dynasty to the beginning of the Western Jin Dynasty. The whole book describes the complex struggle among the Three Kingdoms of Wei, Shu, and Wu. The novel reflects the social contradictions and struggles at that time and portrays a number of heroes, including Cao Cao, Liu Bei, Sun Quan, Zhuge Liang, and Zhou Yu. In grasping the history of the Three Kingdoms, the author shows obvious personal tendency. He appreciates Liu Bei's benevolence and virtue and criticizes Cao Cao's treacherous and sinister ways.

Romance of the Three Kingdoms is very popular in China, and many stories in this novel are well known and have been spread to Japan, the Democratic People's Republic of Korea, the Republic of Korea, Vietnam, Thailand, Russia and other countries.

Three Visits to the Hut

After a great war, Cao Cao defeated Liu Bei. Liu Bei badly needed wise people. One of Liu Bei's staff Xu Shu told him that there was a very smart man named Zhuge Liang in Nanyang. If Liu Bei could get his help, he could rule the whole country.

The next day, Liu Bei, Guan Yu, and Zhang Fei took gifts to visit Zhuge Liang in Nanyang. After a long walk, they finally arrived at a hut. Liu Bei personally dismounted and knocked at the door. A boy opened the door and told

诸葛亮回来了。可是等刘备进去后才知道那个青年是诸葛亮的弟弟。他告诉刘备，哥哥受朋友的邀请外出了，他也不知道什么时候回来。刘备非常失望，只好留下一封信，说自己渴望得到诸葛亮的帮助，平定天下。

过了新年，刘备选了个好日子，第三次来到诸葛亮的家。这一次，诸葛亮正好在睡觉。刘备让关羽、张飞在门外等候，自己在台阶下静静地站着。过了好几个钟头，诸葛亮才醒来，刘备看到诸葛亮气质非凡，心里暗暗高兴。

刘备请求诸葛亮出山，帮助自己平定天下。诸葛亮起初拒绝了刘备，后来经过了与刘备的几次对话，诸葛亮被打动了。他给刘备分析了天下的形势，刘备一听，更加佩服。他们俩聊了整整一晚上。第二天，诸葛亮告别了家人，跟随刘备出发，从此开始了自己传奇的一生。

Liu Bei that Zhuge Liang had gone out. They had to go back. A few days later, Liu Bei, Guanyu and Zhang Fei visited Zhuge Liang again. It was cold and snowy that day. Liu Bei went to the door and heard the sound of reading. Liu Bei thought Zhuge Liang had come back. But when Liu Bei went in, he learned that the sound was from Zhuge Liang's brother and Zhuge Liang had been invited to go out with his friends and no one knew when he would come back. Liu Bei was so disappointed that he had to leave a letter saying that he longed for Zhuge Liang's help to bring peace to the country.

After the New Year, Liu Bei chose a good day and came to Zhuge Liang's home for the third time. This time, Zhuge Liang was sleeping. Liu Bei asked Guan Yu and Zhang Fei to wait outside the door and he himself stood quietly under the steps. After several hours, Zhuge Liang woke up. Liu Bei was very happy to see Zhuge Liang's extraordinary temperament.

Liu Bei asked Zhuge Liang to join him and help to bring peace to the whole country. Zhuge Liang initially refused Liu Bei, but later after several conversations with Liu Bei, Zhuge Liang was moved. He gave Liu Bei an analysis of the country's situation. Liu Bei listened and admired him more. They talked all night. The next day, Zhuge Liang said goodbye to his family, followed Liu Bei and began his legendary life.

草 船 借 箭

曹操的军队非常强大，所以刘备和孙权互相合作，共同抵抗曹操的军队。周瑜是孙权的大将，他看到诸葛亮的聪明才干，心里很妒忌。

有一天，周瑜请诸葛亮讨论军事，说："我们就要跟曹军作战了。请问水上作战用什么兵器最好？"诸葛亮回答："用弓箭最好。"于是周瑜让诸葛亮在十天之内负责造十万支箭，说："这是公事，不能推辞。"诸葛亮告诉周瑜："只要三天。三天造不完，我愿意接受惩罚。"周瑜一听，非常高兴。

鲁肃也是孙权的手下，他和周瑜是非常好的朋友。他来见诸葛亮，诸葛亮对他说："我答应周瑜，三天之内要造十万支箭，我想请你帮忙。"鲁肃说："这是你自己愿意的，我怎么能帮得上你呢？"诸葛亮说："你借给我二十条船，每条船上要三十名军士，还要一千多个稻草人，排在船的两边，第三天自然就有十万支箭了。你不要告诉周瑜，他要是知道了，我的计划就完不成了。"

鲁肃答应了诸葛亮，信守承诺。第一天过去了，周瑜看到诸葛亮没有什么进展；第二天又过去了，周瑜看到诸葛亮仍然没有什么进展。直到第三天凌晨，诸葛亮秘密地把鲁肃请到船里。鲁肃问他："你叫我来做什么？"诸葛亮说："请你一起去取箭。"

Borrowing Arrows with Thatched Boats

Cao Cao's army was very strong, so Liu Bei and Sun Quan cooperated with each other to resist his army. Zhou Yu, the general of Sun Quan, was jealous of Zhuge Liang's intelligence.

One day, Zhou Yu asked Zhuge Liang to discuss military affairs and said, "We are going to fight Cao's army. What is the best weapon for water combat?" Zhuge Liang answered, "It's best to use bows and arrows." So Zhou Yu asked Zhuge Liang to build 100,000 arrows in ten days and said, "This is official business, and you can't refuse it." Zhuge Liang told Zhou Yu, "Three days will be enough. I'm willing to accept punishment if I can't finish it in three days." Zhou Yu was very happy to hear that.

Lu Su was also Sun Quan's subordinate, and he and Zhou Yu were very good friends. When he came to visit Zhuge Liang, Zhuge Liang said to him, "I promise Zhou Yu to build 100,000 arrows in three days. I want to ask you for help." Lu Su said, "This is what you have promised to do. How can I help you?" Zhuge Liang said, "You lend me twenty boats, each with thirty sergeants, and more than a thousand scarecrows on either side of the boat. On the third day, there will naturally be 100,000 arrows. Don't tell Zhou Yu. If he knows, my plan will not be completed."

Lu Su promised Zhuge Liang and kept his promise. When the first day passed, Zhou Yu saw that Zhuge Liang had made little progress; when the second day passed, Zhou Yu saw that Zhuge Liang had done nothing. Until the morning of the third day, Zhuge Liang secretly invited Lu Su into the boat. Lu Su asked him, "What do you need me for?" Zhuge Liang said, "I would like to invite you to go and get the arrows together with me."

　　诸葛亮叫人把二十条船用绳索连接起来。那天的雾很大，天还没亮，人们都看不清远处。当船接近曹操的军队时，诸葛亮下令把船横摆开，又叫船上的军士一边敲鼓，一边大声呼喊。鲁肃吃惊地说："如果曹兵出来，怎么办？"诸葛亮笑了笑，说："雾这样大，曹操一定不敢派兵出来。"诸葛亮果然神机妙算！曹操听到了鼓声，一看江上雾大，没有轻易动兵，而是命令手下朝他们射箭。很快一万多名弓箭手一起朝江中放箭，箭好像下雨一样。不一会儿，船两边的稻草人上都插满了箭。曹操知道自己上了当，想要追诸葛亮的军队，可是那时已经来不及了。

　　鲁肃回去后，告诉了周瑜整个借箭的经过。周瑜叹息了一声，说："诸葛亮神机妙算，我真比不上他！"

Zhuge Liang asked people to connect the twenty boats with ropes. It was very foggy that day. It was still dark and people couldn't see far away. When the boats approached Cao Cao's army, Zhuge Liang ordered the boats to be swayed, and asked the soldiers on the boats to shout aloud while beating drums. Lu Su said in surprise, "What if Cao's army comes out?" Zhuge Liang smiled and said, "The fog is so heavy that Cao Cao must not dare send troops out." This was really a clever idea! Cao Cao heard the drums and, seeing the fog on the river, ordered his men to shoot arrows at them instead of launching troops easily. Soon more than 10,000 archers joined forces to shoot arrows into the river. The arrows seemed to be like a heavy rain. Soon, the scarecrows on both sides of the boats were filled with arrows. Cao Cao knew he was taken in and wanted to catch up with Zhuge Liang's army, but it was too late.

When Lu Su came back, he told Zhou Yu about the whole process of borrowing arrows. Zhou Yu sighed and said, "Zhuge Liang is so shrewd that I really can't compete with him!"

4. 重点词汇

创作

《三国演义》是由谁**创作**的?

拜访

如果你是刘备,去**拜访**诸葛亮时,会带些什么礼物?

妒忌

周瑜为什么**妒忌**诸葛亮?

有智慧的

在你们国家中,有没有跟诸葛亮一样**有智慧的**人?

5. 实践活动

(1)《三国演义》和真实的历史不尽相同,查找资料,看看《三国演义》中的哪些情节跟历史上不太一样。你认为作者为什么要改写?这种改写会产生什么影响?

(2)流行网络游戏"王者荣耀"中,曹操是游戏规则的制定者。在《三国演义》中,曹操是一个奸诈凶残的君主。请查找资料,看看历史上真实的曹操是怎样的人。

4. Keywords

create

Who **created** *Romance of the Three Kingdoms*?

visit

If you were Liu Bei, what gifts would you bring when you **visited** Zhuge Liang?

jealous

Why was Zhou Yu **jealous** of Zhuge Liang?

wise

Are there any **wise** people in your country like Zhuge Liang?

5. Activities

(1) *Romance of the Three Kingdoms* is different from the real history. Look for information and see which plots in *Romance of the Three Kingdoms* are different from those in history. Why do you think the author changed the history in his novel? What impact will this rewriting have?

(2) In the popular online game "King of Glory", Cao Cao is the rule maker of the game. In *Romance of the Three Kingdoms*, Cao Cao is a treacherous and cruel monarch. Look for information and see what kind of person Cao Cao was in history.

（3）《三国演义》中有三位领袖，分别是曹操、刘备和孙权。如果你是三国时期的人，你会选择为哪位领袖服务？为什么？

（4）在《三国演义》中，关羽是刘备的好兄弟，对刘备非常忠心。在中国民间，关羽以"武圣"的头衔和"文圣"孔子平起平坐，人们建关公庙，祈求关公保护。请向同学介绍一下关羽，并且分析为什么关羽会受到百姓的喜爱。

（5）在三国文化中，诸葛亮是贤相的代表，刘备是仁君的代表，关羽是良将的代表。在其他国家文化中，有没有类似的人物？跟三国中的人物比较起来，有哪些异同？

(3) There are three leaders in *Romance of the Three Kingdoms*: Cao Cao, Liu Bei, and Sun Quan. If you were a person in the Three Kingdoms period, which leader would you choose to serve? Why?

(4) In *Romance of the Three Kingdoms*, Guan Yu is Liu Bei's good friend and is very loyal to Liu Bei. For Chinese people, Guan Yu is on an equal footing with Confucius as "Wu Sheng". People build Guan Gong Temple and pray for Guan Gong's protection. Please introduce Guan Yu to your classmates and analyze why he is loved by the people.

(5) In the culture of the Three Kingdoms, Zhuge Liang is the representative of virtuous ministers, Liu Bei is the representative of benevolent emperors, and Guan Yu is the representative of good generals. Are there any similar figures in other cultures? What are the similarities and differences between these figures?

（6）分成小组，根据人物特点，自行编排人物对话，分别扮演刘备、诸葛亮、关羽、张飞、曹操、周瑜和鲁肃等人物，表演经典故事"三顾茅庐"和"草船借箭"。

6. 自我评估

	😊	😐	😞
（1）我能说出《三国演义》的基本情节。			
（2）我能说出《三国演义》的主要人物及其特点。			
（3）我能讲述《三国演义》中的一两个经典故事。			

(6) In groups, arrange the dialogues according to the characteristics of the characters. You can act as Liu Bei, Zhuge Liang, Guan Yu, Zhang Fei, Cao Cao, Zhou Yu, and Lu Su respectively and perform the classic stories of "Three Visits to the Hut" and "Borrowing Arrows with Thatched Boats".

6. Self-assessment

	🙂	😐	🙁
(1) I can tell the basic plot of *Romance of the Three Kingdoms*.			
(2) I can tell the main characters of *Romance of the Three Kingdoms* and their characteristics.			
(3) I can tell one or two classic stories in *Romance of the Three Kingdoms*.			

第九课　全民健身

1. 学习目标

（1）了解全民健身的含义。

（2）能向朋友介绍中国现代流行的运动项目。

（3）能比较中外体育运动的异同。

2. 热身活动

讨论

（1）说起"健身"，你会想到哪些运动？

（2）你和家人喜欢运动吗？你最喜欢什么运动？通常在哪里运动？

（3）你认为2008年北京奥运会给中国人的生活方式带来了哪些改变？中国为什么要提出"全民健身"？

（4）你认为中国人和其他国家的人的运动方式有哪些异同？

Lesson Nine   National Fitness

1. Learning objectives

(1) Know the meaning of national fitness.

(2) Be able to introduce to friends the popular modern sports in China.

(3) Be able to tell the similarities and differences between Chinese and others' sports.

2. Warm-up

Discussion

(1) When it comes to fitness, what sports do you think of?

(2) Do you and your family like sports? What's your favorite sport? Where do you usually exercise?

(3) What changes do you think the 2008 Beijing Olympic Games have brought to the Chinese people's lifestyle? Why does China propose "national fitness"?

(4) What do you think are the similarities and differences between Chinese and others' ways of exercise?

3. 阅读课文

全民健身简介

2008年北京成功举办奥运会，让更多的中国人爱上了体育和健身。为了纪念北京奥运会成功举办，中国将每年的8月8日设置为"全民健身日"。全民健身是指全国人民，不分男女老少，共同参加各种形式的锻炼，从而达到身体强健的目的。政府倡导每个人每天都参加一次以上的体育健身活动，学会两种以上的健身方法，每年进行一次体质测定。全民健身是中国体育工作的重要内容，是实现全民健康的重要途径和手段。

中国人爱上了跑步

最近几年，参与跑步运动的中国人呈现大幅增长。在社交网络上晒跑步成绩成了很多人每天的习惯。在北京的奥林匹克森林公园、上海的世纪公园、厦门的环岛路，以及身边的公园小径、社区道路上，到处都可以看到跑步的人们。

跑步人数的增长带动了国内马拉松赛事的火爆。2014年9月的上海马拉松，18,000个参赛名额在几个小时内就被一扫而空，网友调侃为"比春运抢票还

3. Reading texts

Introduction to National Fitness

In 2008, Beijing successfully hosted the Olympic Games, which made more Chinese people like sports and fitness. In order to commemorate the successful hosting of the Beijing Olympic Games, the Chinese government set August 8 as "National Fitness Day". National fitness means that people of the whole country, regardless of gender and age, jointly participate in various forms of exercise, so as to achieve the goal of physical fitness. The government advocates that everyone takes part in more than one physical fitness activity every day, learns more than two methods of physical fitness, and conducts a physical fitness test every year. National fitness is an important part of China's sports work and an important way to achieve national health.

Chinese People Like Running

In recent years, the number of Chinese people participating in running has increased dramatically. Posting running results on social networks has become a daily habit of many people. Runners can be seen everywhere, such as Beijing's Olympic Forest Park, Shanghai's Century Park, and Xiamen's Huandao Road, as well as some park trails and community roads.

The increase in the number of runners has boosted the domestic marathon races. In the Shanghai Marathon in September 2014, 18,000 entries were swept away within a few hours. Netizens joked that it was "harder than grabbing tickets

难"；而在1个月后的北京马拉松，因报名人数太多，不得不摇号确定参赛资格，根据相关报道，中签率只有14.2%。

而2014年前，如果一个马拉松赛开放报名，主办方需要以赠送运动装、跑鞋等礼品，到大专院校去宣传等方式来吸引人们报名；而现在，到处有报不上名的人想方设法来求参赛名额。为什么跑步变得很流行了呢？

首先是因为人们的生活水平提高了。2012年中国人均GDP达到5,400美元。研究表明，当人均GDP突破5,000美元这条线后，人们对于娱乐、生活方式、生活品质的要求会多起来，消遣、休闲、健身这类享受型消费在居民消费中所占的比重会越来越大。也就是说，越来越多的中国人开始有条件追求健康的生活方式。

第二，跑步是最方便的运动方式。它没有什么场地、器械的特别要求，没有性别年龄、时间限制，挑一双合适的跑鞋，学习一下正确的跑步姿势，速度可快可慢，路程可长可短，自由度极高。

第三，网络软件的出现也推动了跑步的发展。2012年，耐克公司和苹果合作推出了手机应用程度Nike Running，鼓励跑步者将运动数据分享到社交网络服务（SNS）平台上。一项运动就这样被转换成社交行为，如果现在让跑步者

for the Spring Festival Rush". In the Beijing Marathon one month later, due to the large number of applicants, the eligibility had to be determined by lottery. According to relevant reports, the winning rate was only 14.2%.

Before 2014, if a marathon is open for registration, the organizers need to attract people to sign up by presenting gifts such as sports clothes and running shoes, and going to colleges and universities to publicize them. Now, there are people everywhere who have no chance to register and try their best to find places to compete. Why has running become so popular?

The first reason is that people's living standards have improved. China's GDP per capita reached $5,400 in 2012. Research shows that when per capita GDP exceeds $5,000, people will have more demands for entertainment, lifestyle and quality of life. Enjoyable consumption such as recreation, leisure and fitness will account for more and more of the residents' consumption. That is to say, more and more Chinese people begin to pursue a healthy lifestyle.

Second, running is the most convenient way to exercise. It needs no special requirements for venues and equipment, and it has no gender, age, or time limit. You can choose a suitable pair of running shoes, and learn the correct running posture. Your speed can be high or low, the distance can be long or short, and you have a high degree of freedom.

Thirdly, the emergence of network software has also promoted the development of running. In 2012, Nike and Apple launched mobile application Nike Running, encouraging runners to share sports data on the Social Networking Services (SNS) platform. A sport has thus been transformed into social behavior, and if runners are now asked to put down their mobile phones for

放下手机，来一场不为人知的马拉松，相信很多人都会拒绝的。

如今，跑步在中国不仅仅是一种锻炼方式，它更是时尚，是新的社交和生活方式，它改变着参与者的生活和精神面貌。

中国现代流行运动

随着社会的发展和全民健身的提出，人们的业余生活越来越丰富，体育运动也更加多样化。人们的选择不再局限于传统的跑步和球类运动。

（1）骑行

走在街上，你总能看到戴着头盔的骑行爱好者。他们来自各个年龄段，无论是对青年人还是中年人，骑行都有着独特的魅力。骑行是一种简单又环保的运动，在骑行的过程中，你既可以欣赏沿途的美景，也可以在路上认识不同的人。

an unknown marathon, it is believed that many of them will refuse to do so.

Today, running is not only a form of exercise in China, but also a fashion. It is a new lifestyle. It changes the participants' life and spiritual outlook.

Popular Modern Sports in China

With the development of society and the proposal of national fitness, people's leisure life is more and more abundant, and sports are more diversified. People's choices are no longer limited to traditional running and ball games.

(1) Cycling

Walking on the street, you can always see cyclists who wear helmets. They come from all ages. Whether they are young or middle-aged, cycling has a unique charm for them. Cycling is a simple and environmentally friendly sport. In the process of cycling, you can both enjoy the beautiful scenery, and meet different people on the way.

（2）国标舞

国标舞，又叫国际标准舞，来源于各个国家的民间舞蹈。国标舞有很多种类，人们比较熟悉的有华尔兹、探戈、伦巴和恰恰等。国标舞的形式一般是两人组合，跳国标舞，人们不仅可以享受优美的音乐，健身，还可以结交朋友。

(2) Ballroom Dancing

Ballroom dancing, also known as international standard ballroom dancing, comes from folk dances of various countries. There are many kinds of ballroom dancing. People are familiar with waltz, tango, rumba, and cha-cha. Ballroom dancing is usually performed by two people. Dancers can not only enjoy beautiful music and fitness, but also make friends.

（3）健身房

如今越来越多的年轻人选择下班后去健身房健身。健身房似乎已经成了时尚和现代的标志。不仅如此，中老年人也意识到健康的重要性，与其把钱花在医院，他们更愿意花钱办张健身卡去健身房运动。

（4）户外运动

谈到户外运动，不得不说的项目就是滑板。滑板在中国的发展起步较晚，但发展非常迅速，尤其受到年轻人的喜爱。滑板既可以作为一种代步工具，也是一种表现个性的时尚追求。越来越多的女孩子也喜欢玩滑板，享受滑板带来的自由。

(3) The Gym

Nowadays, more and more young people choose to go to the gym after work. The gym seems to have become a symbol of fashion and being modern. Middle-aged people and elderly people are also aware of the importance of health. Instead of spending money on hospitals, they prefer to spend money on a fitness card to go to the gym.

(4) Outdoor Sports

When it comes to outdoor sports, we have to mention skateboarding. Skateboarding started late in China, but it developed very rapidly, especially among young people. The skateboard can not only be used as a means of transport, but also a fashion pursuit to express personality. More and more girls also like to play skateboarding and enjoy the freedom it brings to them.

（5）极限运动

在现代社会，人们的生活节奏加快，工作压力也越来越大，一些人为了追求新的刺激，不断尝试高难度、高风险的极限运动。极限运动的种类很多，人们比较熟悉的有攀岩、极限越野、冲浪、蹦极、跑酷、潜水等。极限运动是现代人对身心的一种挑战，是对自我极限的不断更新，人们在超越自我中获得了满足感和愉悦感。

4. 重点词汇

健身

中国人最常见的**健身**方式有哪些？

(5) Extreme Sports

In modern society, people's life pace is speeding up, and the pressure of work is increasing. In order to pursue new stimulation, some people constantly try more difficult and high-risk sports. There are many kinds of extreme sports. People are familiar with rock climbing, extreme cross-country, surfing, bungee jumping, parkour, diving, and so on. Extreme sports are challenges to the body and mind of modern people, and also the constant renewal of self-limit. People get a sense of satisfaction and pleasure in transcending themselves.

4. Keywords

keep fit

What are the most common ways for Chinese people to **keep fit**?

怎么样可以保持身体**健康**?

你会参加**马拉松**比赛吗?

为什么滑板、冲浪被认为是**极限运动**?

5. 实践活动

（1）有人说"中国是体育强国，但不是体育大国"，你同意吗？请结合下图谈谈你的看法。

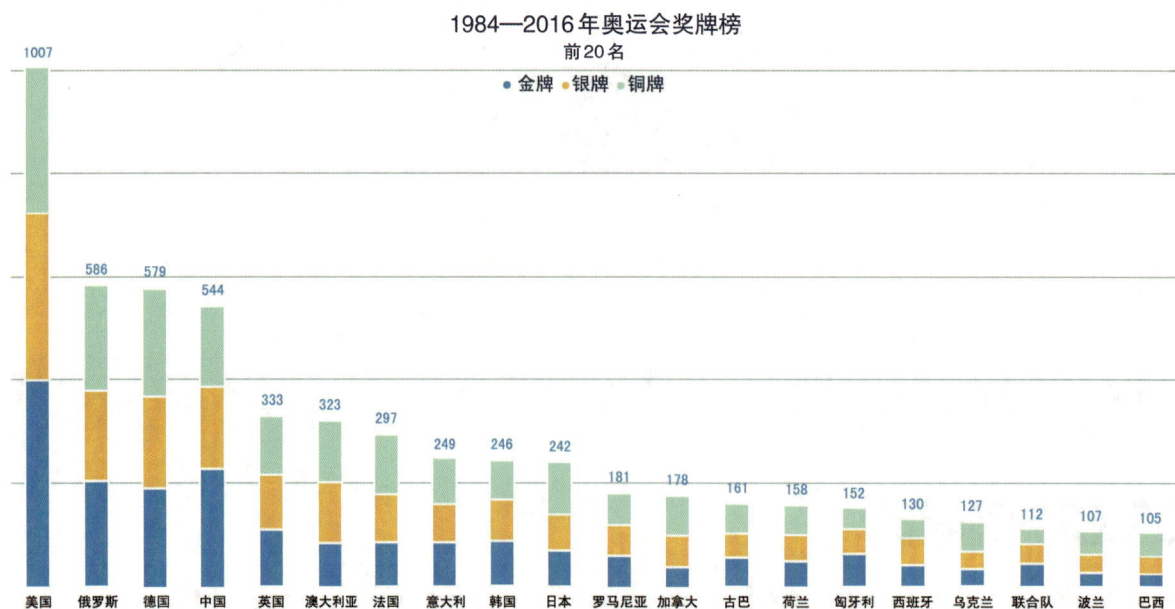

1984—2016 年奥运会奖牌榜
前 20 名

● 金牌 ● 银牌 ● 铜牌

美国	俄罗斯	德国	中国	英国	澳大利亚	法国	意大利	韩国	日本	罗马尼亚	加拿大	古巴	荷兰	匈牙利	西班牙	乌克兰	联合队	波兰	巴西
1007	586	579	544	333	323	297	249	246	242	181	178	161	158	152	130	127	112	107	105

health

How to keep **healthy**?

marathon

Will you take part in the **marathon**?

extreme sports

Why are skateboarding and surfing considered as **extreme sports**?

5. Activities

(1) Some people say that China is a leading sports nation, but not a major sports country. Do you agree? Please share your views based on the picture below.

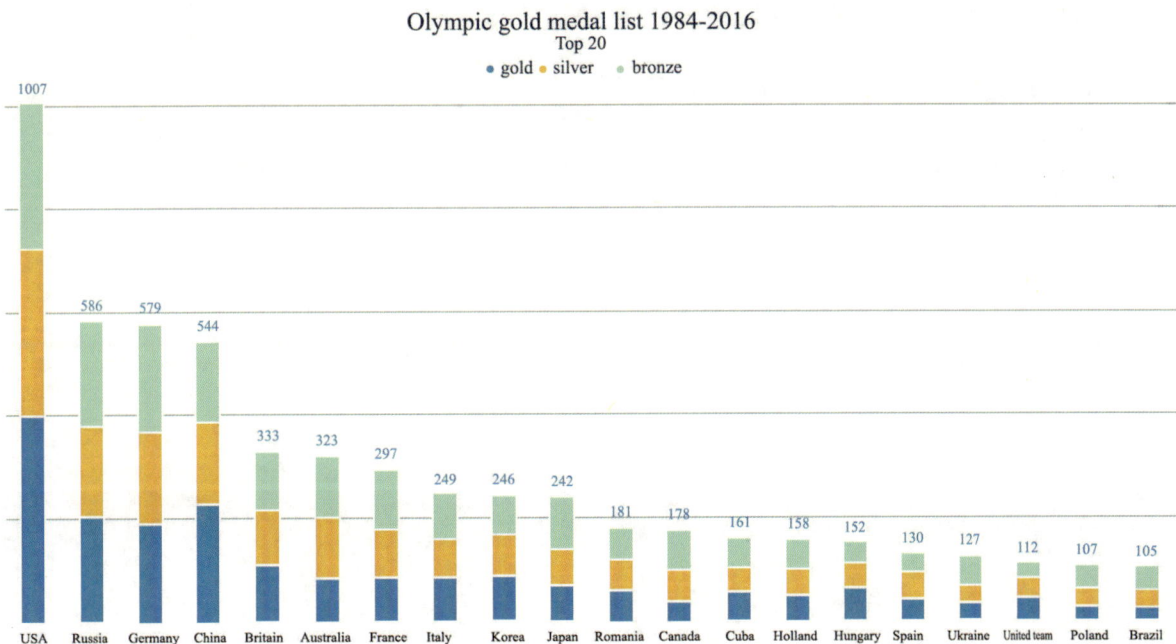

Olympic gold medal list 1984-2016
Top 20
● gold ● silver ● bronze

USA	Russia	Germany	China	Britain	Australia	France	Italy	Korea	Japan	Romania	Canada	Cuba	Holland	Hungary	Spain	Ukraine	United team	Poland	Brazil
1007	586	579	544	333	323	297	249	246	242	181	178	161	158	152	130	127	112	107	105

（2）你有没有看过中国人跳广场舞？请访问一下跳舞的人，问问他们为什么会参加这项活动。

（3）做一个调查，了解人们平时健身选择什么运动，以及他们为什么想要健身。整理采访内容并总结汇报。说说你认为的最好的健身方式。

（4）如果你要去运动，你会选择什么地方？参加什么运动？为什么？

（5）体育健身运动的发展对中国的经济也产生了很大的影响，请查找资料，介绍一下中国体育产业的发展。

（6）如果你要组织一个运动社团，你会选择什么项目？为什么？

6. 自我评估

	😊	😐	😞
（1）我能说出全民健身的含义。			
（2）我能说出一些中国现代流行运动的种类。			
（3）我参与了一项中国流行健身方式。			

(2) Have you ever seen Chinese people square dancing? Please interview the dancers and ask why they take part in this activity.

(3) Do a survey to find out what kinds of sports people usually choose to do and why they want to exercise. Collect the interview content and summarize the report. Tell us what you think is the best way to keep fit.

(4) If you are going to exercise, where will you choose? What sports will you take part in? Why?

(5) The development of sports and fitness also has a great impact on China's economy. Please look for information and introduce the development of China's sports industry.

(6) If you want to organize a sports club, what events will you choose? Why?

6. Self-assessment

	☺	😐	☹
(1) I can tell the meaning of national fitness.			
(2) I can name some kinds of popular modern sports in China.			
(3) I have participated in a popular fitness program in China.			

第十课　中国少数民族

1. 学习目标

（1）能说出中国少数民族的分布特点。

（2）能说出中国一两个少数民族的风俗习惯。

（3）能简单说明中国的民族政策。

2. 热身活动

讨论

（1）中国到处都有"清真"字样的餐厅，这是什么意思？

（2）中国有多少少数民族？人口最多的少数民族是哪个？

（3）你见过中国少数民族吗？你印象中的少数民族是什么样的？

（4）你们国家是由单一民族组成还是由多民族组成？请简单介绍一下。

Lesson Ten   Ethnic Minority Groups in China

1. Learning objectives

(1) Be able to describe the distribution features of ethnic minority groups in China.

(2) Be able to talk about the customs of one to two ethnic minority groups in China.

(3) Be able to give a brief account of China's ethnic policy.

2. Warm-up

Discussion

(1) There are restaurants with the word "Qingzhen" in their names everywhere in China. What does that mean?

(2) How many ethnic minority groups are there in China? Which is the most populous?

(3) Have you ever seen ethnic minority groups in China? What is your impression of them?

(4) Is your country a monoethnic country or a multiethnic country? Please give a brief introduction to it.

3. 阅读课文

中国少数民族及其分布

中国是一个多民族的国家，在这片广大的土地上，一共有五十六个民族。

五十六个民族中，汉族人数最多，占全国人口的91.11%，五十五个少数民族占全国人口的8.89%。其中，满族、蒙古族、回族、藏族的人数在少数民族中占比很高，是少数民族中人数较多的四个民族。虽然少数民族的总人数不到全国人口的十分之一，其分布却十分广泛，所生活的地区也比汉族要广大。中国少数民族人口的分布主要有两个特点：

第一，大杂居小聚居。中国设置了内蒙古、新疆、西藏、广西、宁夏五个少数民族自治区，以及许许多多的自治州、自治县和民族乡。在这些自治的区域里，人民群众大多以民族为单位，聚集起来居住。同时，在这些地区，汉族

3. Reading texts

Ethnic Minority Groups in China and Their Distribution

China is a multiethnic country. There are 56 nationalities in this vast land.

Among the 56 nationalities, the Han nationality accounts for 91.11% of the national population, and the 55 ethnic minority groups account for 8.89% of the national population. Among them, the Manchu, Mongol, Hui, and Tibetan nationalities account for a high proportion of the ethnic minority population, and they are the four ethnic minority groups with a comparatively larger number of people. Although the total number of ethnic minority groups is less than one tenth of the national population, they are widely distributed and live in larger areas than the Han nationality. The distribution of ethnic minority groups in China has two main characteristics:

Firstly, they live together in both large and small communities. China has set up five autonomous regions of ethnic minority groups—Inner Mongolia, Xinjiang, Tibet, Guangxi, and Ningxia, as well as numerous autonomous prefectures, autonomous counties, and ethnic townships. In these autonomous regions,

人民的比例也比较高。同样，在汉族人主要居住的地区也杂居着不少少数民族。民族杂居成了中国民族居住的常态。

第二，分布范围广，主要集中于西部及边疆地区。少数民族主要居住在中国的西南、西北和东北各处。中国有29个民族遍布全国所有省区，拥有56个民族的省区有11个。云南是中国少数民族最多的省份，有25个少数民族居住在这片西南仙境中。然而，少数民族的人口仍主要集中在西部及边疆地区，特别是广西、云南、贵州、新疆四个省区的少数民族人口之和占全国少数民族人口的一半以上。

中国少数民族的服饰

中国多样的自然环境和生活方式塑造了各个少数民族不同的民族性格和民族心理，也造成了各个少数民族不同的服饰风格和服饰特点。

在中国北方地区，气温多变，人口稀少，畜牧业成了这里主要的生产方式。因此，生活在这里的少数民族大多身穿宽袍大袖、厚实庄重的衣物。他们大多取用牲畜皮毛作为缝制衣物的原料。譬如人口排名第九的蒙古族和充满魅力的

most of the people gather and live in ethnic units. Moreover, the proportion of the Han nationality in these areas is relatively high. Similarly, there are many ethnic minority groups living in the areas where the Han nationality lives. Ethnic cohabitation has become the norm of ethnic residence in China.

Secondly, they are widely distributed, mainly in the western and frontier areas. The ethnic minority groups mainly live in the southwest, northwest, and northeast of China. China has 29 nationalities in all provinces and autonomous regions, and there are 11 provinces and autonomous regions with 56 nationalities. Yunnan is the province with the largest number of ethnic minority groups in China. There are 25 ethnic minority groups living in this southwestern fairyland. However, the population of ethnic minority groups is still concentrated in the western and frontier areas, especially in Guangxi, Yunnan, Guizhou, and Xinjiang. The total population of ethnic minority groups there accounts for more than half of the national ethnic minority population.

Costumes of the Ethnic Minority Groups in China

China's diverse natural environment and lifestyle shape the character and psychology of different ethnic minority groups, and also inspire different costume styles and characteristics of them.

In northern China, where the temperature is changeable and the population is scarce, animal husbandry has become the main mode of production. Therefore, most of the ethnic minority groups living here like to wear wide-sleeved gowns and heavy and solemn clothes. Most of them use animal fur as raw material for sewing clothes. For example, the Mongol nationality, the

哈萨克族就多以毛饰构成自己的服饰风格。这样一来，暖和的动物皮毛能帮他们抵御冬季的寒冷，而在夏季，他们就卸掉厚重的毛饰，独特而美丽的帽子则可以抵挡住强烈的日光照射。

而在中国南方，少数民族居住的地区大多气候炎热，且人们也不以畜牧为生，而多是从事植麻种棉。因此，南方少数民族服装的主要面料是自织麻布和土布，并且织物精美，花纹美丽。因为气候原因，他们的衣裙也大多短窄轻薄。不同

ninth largest population in the country, and the Kazak nationality, which is full of charm, make up their own dress style mostly with wool ornaments. In this way, warm animal fur can help them withstand the cold in winter, and in summer, they remove the heavy fur, and the unique and beautiful hats can withstand the strong sunlight.

In southern China, most of the areas inhabited by ethnic minority groups have hot climate, and people there do not live on animal husbandry, but are mostly engaged in planting hemp and cotton. Therefore, the main fabrics of their costumes are self-woven linen and homespun cloth, and the fabrics are exquisite with beautiful patterns. Because of the hot climate, most of their clothes and skirts are short, narrow,

于北方的厚重，南方少数民族的服饰风格生动活泼，式样繁多，却各不相同。譬如壮族、苗族、白族等，都以自身服饰上多彩的纹路和精致的饰品展现着他们/她们令人着迷的魅力。

中国少数民族的风俗习惯

中国的少数民族大多能歌善舞，每个少数民族的风俗不尽相同。中国人对食物有着极大的热情，在如何做饭方面，每个少数民族都有自己独特的风俗。佤族、黎族有名的竹筒饭，就是用竹筒做饭，因此做出的饭带有新竹的清香；而游牧民族常常用青稞、燕麦等做炒面，并用牲畜做烤肉；维吾尔族喜欢将面粉、玉米烤成馕，还常用羊肉、胡萝卜、洋葱和大米做成米饭，捏团抓食，这就是我们所说的"抓饭"。

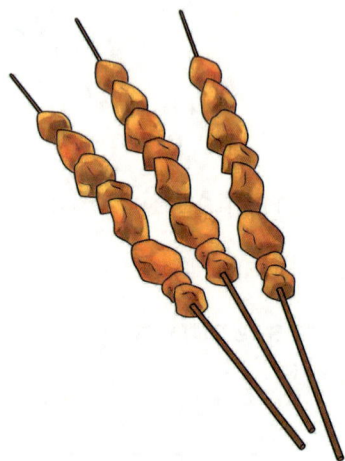

and light. Different from the thick and heavy costumes in the north, those in the south are lively and varied. For example, the Zhuang, Miao, and Bai nationalities show their fascinating charm with the colorful patterns and exquisite ornaments on their clothes.

The Customs of Ethnic Minority Groups in China

Most ethnic minority groups in China are good at singing and dancing, and their customs are different from each other. Chinese people have great enthusiasm for food. Every ethnic minority group has its own unique cooking customs. The Wa and Li nationalities are famous for bamboo tubular rice, which is cooked with bamboo tubular, so the meal is fragrant with new bamboo. The nomads often use barley, oats to make fried noodles, and use livestock as barbecue. The Uygur nationality likes to bake flour and corn into steamed bread, and often uses mutton, carrots, onions, and rice to make "grabbing rice".

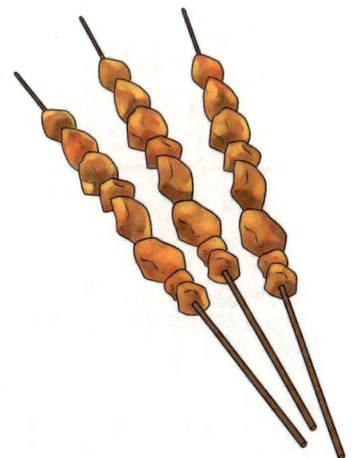

　　中国的少数民族还有很多自己的节日。比如，傣族有泼水节、蒙古族有那达慕。泼水节是傣族的新年，一般持续3至7天。节日期间，不分男女老少，可以互相泼水，表示洗旧迎新之意。很多人喜欢整桶整盆地泼，甚至用水龙管喷浇。人们被泼得越多越高兴，因为水象征着幸福。在蒙古语中，"那达慕"的意思是"游戏"或"娱乐"，原指蒙古族传统的"男子三竞技"：摔跤、赛马和射箭。随着时代的发展，逐渐演变成包括多种文化娱乐内容的盛大庆典活动和物资交流活动。

中国的民族政策

　　针对多民族的国情，中国政府制定了一套适合中国国情的方针和政策。这就是民族平等、民族团结、民族区域自治和各民族共同发展，民族平等是中国民族政策的核心。中国政府也将民族区域自治作为中国的一项重要政治制度。目前，已建立了内蒙古自治区、新疆维吾尔自治区、广西壮族自治区、宁夏回

The ethnic minority groups in China also have many of their own festivals. For example, the Water-Splashing Festival of the Dai nationality and the Nadam Fair of the Mongol nationality. The Water-Splashing Festival is the New Year of the Dai nationality, which usually lasts for three to seven days. During the festival, people of all ages splash water on each other to express the meaning of washing the old and welcoming the new. Many people like to pour a full bucket or basin of water to others, and even spray them with hoses. The more people are thrown with water, the happier they will be, because water symbolizes happiness. In Mongolian, "Nadam" means "game" or "entertainment", originally referring to Mongolian traditional "three men's competitions": wrestling, horse racing, and archery. With the passage of times, it has gradually evolved into grand celebration and commodity trading activities which include various cultural and entertainment contents.

China's Ethnic Policy

In view of the multiethnic situation, the Chinese government has formulated a set of guidelines and policies suited to China's national conditions. These are the ethnic policies in the principles of ethnic equality and unity, regional ethnic autonomy, and the common prosperity of all ethnic groups. Ethnic equality is the core of China's ethnic policy. The Chinese government also regards the system of regional ethnic autonomy as an important political system in China. At present, Inner Mongolia Autonomous Region, Xinjiang Uygur Autonomous Region, Guangxi Zhuang Autonomous Region, Ningxia Hui

族自治区和西藏自治区以及若干地方自治政府。这样各民族便可以根据自身的情况，合理进行自行管理，从而避免了许多冲突与纠纷。因此，中国各民族形成了平等、团结、互助的友好民族关系。

4. 重点词汇

少数民族

中国的**少数民族**占总人口的比例是多少？

杂居

"**大杂居**"是什么意思？

自治区

中国一共有多少个少数民族**自治区**？

风俗

你能介绍一个你们国家的节日**风俗**吗？

平等

男女**平等**很重要。

Autonomous Region, Tibet Autonomous Region, and some local autonomous governments have been established. In this way, all nationalities can manage themselves reasonably according to their own conditions, thus avoiding many conflicts and disputes. Therefore, all nationalities in China have formed friendly relations of equality, unity, and mutual assistance.

4. Keywords

ethnic minority group

What is the proportion of **ethnic minority groups** in the total population of China?

ethnic cohabitation

What does "big **ethnic cohabitation**" mean?

autonomous region

How many **autonomous regions** of ethnic minority groups are there in China?

custom

Can you introduce a festival **custom** in your country?

equality

Gender **equality** is an important issue.

5. 实践活动

（1）下列图片分别代表中国的哪个民族？

（2）根据下面两幅图，说说传统旗袍和现代旗袍分别有哪些不同。

（3）中国的少数民族中有一个"回族"。请查阅资料，研究一下这个民族的产生和演变历史，向同学介绍一下。

5. Activities

(1) Look at the pictures below. What ethnic minority groups in China do they represent?

(2) Look at the following traditional cheongsam and modern cheongsam, and analyze their differences.

(3) Among the ethnic minority groups in China, there is the Hui nationality. Please look for information about the emergence and evolution of this nationality, and introduce it to your classmates.

（4）查找资料，向同学介绍一下中国的民族区域自治政策包括哪些具体内容。

（5）如果你去新疆或者西藏旅行，跟当地人交流时，需要注意什么？

（6）如果有条件，可以参观少数民族服饰展览，并说一下哪个少数民族给你留下了深刻印象。

6. 自我评估

	😊	😐	😞
（1）我能说出中国少数民族的分布特点。			
（2）我能说出中国一两个少数民族的风俗习惯。			
（3）我能简单说出中国的民族政策。			

【附录】55个中国少数民族名称

阿昌族、白族、保安族、布朗族、布依族、朝鲜族、达斡尔族、傣族、德昂族、东乡族、侗族、独龙族、俄罗斯族、鄂伦春族、鄂温克族、高山族、仡佬族、哈尼族、哈萨克族、赫哲族、回族、基诺族、京族、景颇族、柯尔克孜族、拉祜族、黎族、傈僳族、珞巴族、满族、毛南族、门巴族、蒙古族、苗族、仫佬族、纳西族、怒族、普米族、羌族、撒拉族、畲族、水族、塔吉克族、塔塔尔族、土家族、土族、佤族、维吾尔族、乌孜别克族、锡伯族、瑶族、彝族、裕固族、藏族、壮族

(4) Look for information and introduce to your classmates the specific contents of China's policy of regional ethnic autonomy.

(5) If you travel to Xinjiang or Tibet and communicate with the local people, what should you pay attention to?

(6) If possible, visit the costume exhibition of the ethnic minority groups, and tell which ethnic minority group impresses you deeply.

6. Self-assessment

	🙂	😐	☹️
(1) I can tell the characteristics of the distribution of ethnic minority groups in China.			
(2) I can tell the customs of one or two ethnic minority groups in China.			
(3) I can give a brief account of China's ethnic policy.			

【Appendix】 Names of the 55 Ethnic Minority Groups in China

Achang, Bai, Bonan, Blang, Bouyei, Korean, Daur, Dai, De'ang, Dongxiang, Dong, Derung, Russian, Oroqen, Ewenki, Gaoshan, Gelao, Hani, Kazak, Hezhen, Hui, Jino, Gin, Jingpo, Kirgiz, Lahu, Li, Lisu, Lhoba, Manchu, Maonan, Monba, Mongol, Miao, Mulao, Naxi, Nu, Pumi, Qiang, Salar, She, Shui, Tajik, Tatar, Tujia, Tu, Va, Uygur, Uzbek, Xibe, Yao, Yi, Yugur, Tibetan, Zhuang

第十一课　汉字印刷

1. 学习目标

（1）能说出中国古代印刷术的发展情况。

（2）能说出活字印刷与雕版印刷的区别。

（3）知道汉字激光照排的意义。

（4）会使用一种汉字输入法输入汉字。

2. 热身活动

讨论

（1）中国的四大发明有哪些?

（2）谁是中国古代印刷术的发明者?

（3）中国人如何在电脑和手机上输入汉字?

（4）如果不会拼音，怎么在电脑和手机上输入汉字?

3. 阅读课文

印刷术的由来

印刷术是中国古代四大发明之一。很早以前，人们只能靠手抄书籍，才能

Lesson Eleven　Chinese Character Printing

1. Learning objectives

(1) Be able to describe the development of printing in ancient China.

(2) Be able to tell the differences between movable-type printing and engraving printing.

(3) Know the meaning of laser phototypesetting of Chinese characters.

(4) Know how to input Chinese characters by using a Chinese input method.

2. Warm-up

Discussion

(1) What are the Four Great Inventions of China?

(2) Who was the inventor of ancient Chinese printing?

(3) How do Chinese people input Chinese characters on computers and cell phones?

(4) If you know nothing about pinyin, how can you input Chinese characters on the computers and cell phones?

3. Reading texts

The Origin of Printing

Printing is one of the Four Great Inventions of ancient China. Long

记录下需要传播的知识。然而，手抄的方式不仅费时费力，又容易抄错抄漏。到了中国唐朝，人们为了节省人力，发明了雕版印刷术，把要印刷的字提前刻在木板上，用刷子在板子上刷上墨，再把纸覆盖在板子上轻轻刷一遍，一页纸就印好了。这种方法大大加快了知识、文化的传播速度。

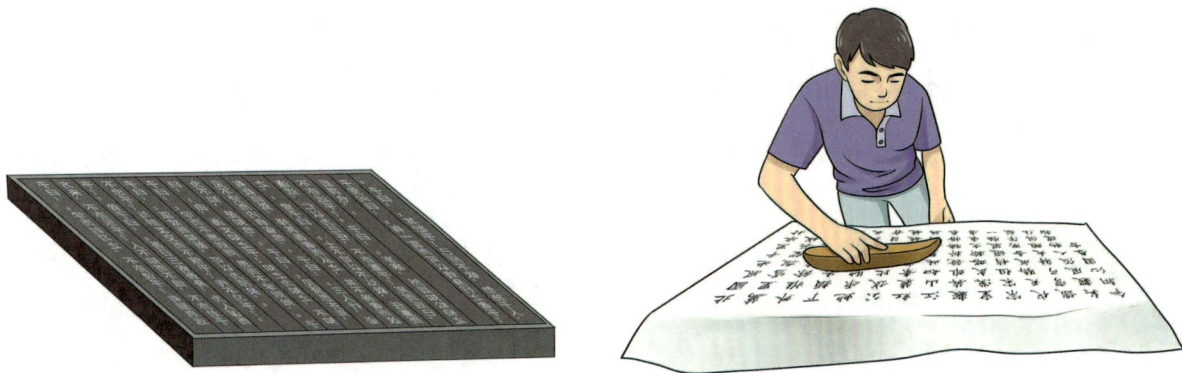

然而人们渐渐发现，雕版印刷术虽然快，可是制作原版模型的过程也非常费力。北宋时期，一位名叫毕昇（972-1051）的人用胶泥做成长方体，在一面刻上单字，再用火烧硬，使得一个印上就有一个字。从此活字印刷术就诞生了。这样的印刷技术比雕版印刷术灵活得多，人们也更容易操作字印，随意印出自己想印的书籍。使用活字印刷的时候，需要预先排版，在一块铁板上围好铁框，并在铁框内摆放要印的字印，就可以进行印刷了。

ago, people hand-copied books to record the knowledge that needed to be disseminated. However, the way of hand-copying is not only time-consuming and laborious, but also easy to commit errors and omissions. In the Tang Dynasty, to save manpower, people invented engraving printing. They carved the characters to be printed on the board, brushed the ink on the board, covered the board with paper, and then pressed it gently and one page of paper was printed. This method has greatly accelerated the dissemination of knowledge and culture.

However, it is gradually found that although engraving printing was fast, the process of making the model was laborious. During the Northern Song Dynasty, a man named Bi Sheng (972–1051) made a cuboid out of plaster, engraved a character on one side, and then burned it, so that one character was printed on it. Thus, movable-type printing was invented. This kind of printing technology was much more flexible than engraving printing, and it was also easier to operate as people could print books they like at will. When using movable-type printing, it is necessary to pre-type, surround the iron frame on a piece of iron plate, and place the prints to be printed in frame so printing can be carried out.

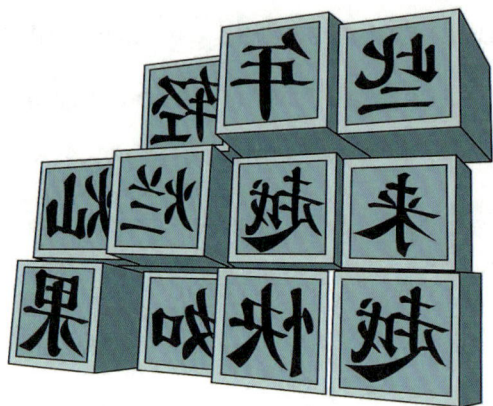

中国的印刷术经过雕版和活字印刷两个阶段的发展，变得越来越成熟，在后来还出现了多色套印、木活字印刷等技术，实现了古代印刷术的重大突破。世界上不少国家的印刷术也是由中国传入，或是受到中国影响发展起来的。2010年11月15日，活字印刷术被列入联合国急需保护的非物质文化遗产名录，足见中国古代文明为世界文明作出的贡献。

After the development of engraving and movable-type printing, Chinese printing has become more mature. Multi-color process printing, wood movable-type printing, and other technologies emerged later, which achieved a major breakthrough in ancient printing. Printing in many countries of the world was also introduced from China or developed under the influence of China. On November 15, 2010, movable-type printing was included in United Nations' list of intangible cultural heritage in urgent need of protection, which shows the contribution of ancient Chinese civilization to world civilization.

激光照排与汉字印刷

活字印刷使得书籍出版、报纸印刷得到了迅速的发展。但是随着电子技术的发展，传统的铅字排版技术显得落后了。为了解决这一问题，人们将目光投向了电子排版技术的研究。1979年，北京大学计算机研究所王选教授带领的科研人员成功研制了独特的激光照排系统，并且在极短的时间里制作出了一张排版复杂的报纸样本。这种电子排版技术彻底改变了中文排版印刷系统，被称为"中国印刷界的革命"。

1981年，王选教授进一步研制出了华光微型机排版系统。这套全新的系统能够输出美观规范的排版，而且方便易学，大大提高了印刷的效率，比古老的印刷功效至少高5倍。到1993年，中国国产的激光照排系统已经占领了99%的中国报业市场和90%的书刊市场，并且被日本和韩国引进。在20世纪末，中国全国的报纸和出版社已经全部采用了激光照排技术。如今，中国绝大多数的报纸、杂志和书籍都在使用着这套系统，同时，它也是世界汉字印刷系统中的领衔设备。而王选教授对汉字激光照排系统的发明，彻底让古老的中国印刷术"告

Laser Phototypesetting and Chinese Character Printing

Movable-type printing enabled book publishing and newspaper printing to develop rapidly. However, with the development of electronic technology, the traditional typesetting technology is lagging behind. In order to solve this problem, people focus on the research of electronic typesetting technology. In 1979, researchers led by Professor Wang Xuan from Institute of Computer Technology, Peking University, successfully developed a unique laser phototypesetting system, and in a very short time produced a complex newspaper sample. This electronic typesetting technology has completely changed the Chinese typesetting and printing system, known as the "Chinese printing revolution".

In 1981, Professor Wang further developed the Huaguang Microcomputer typesetting system. This new system, which can output beautiful and standard typesetting and is easy to learn, has greatly improved the efficiency of printing, making it at least five times more effective than older printing methods. By 1993, China's domestic laser phototypesetting system had occupied 99% of China's newspaper market and 90% of the book market, and was introduced to Japan and the Republic of Korea. By the end of the 20th century, all newspapers and publishing houses in China had adopted laser phototypesetting technology. Nowadays, most newspapers, magazines, and books in China are using this system. At the same time, it is also the leading equipment in the world's Chinese printing system. Professor Wang's invention of the laser phototypesetting system of Chinese characters has made the ancient Chinese printing "farewell to the lead and fire, and usher in light and electricity", making it more convenient for the Chinese character cultural system to go to the world. Professor Wang has been

别铅与火，迎来光与电"，让汉字文化系统更方便地走向世界。王选教授获得了中国十大科技成就奖和国家技术进步一等奖，并获得1987年我国首次设立的印刷界个人最高荣誉奖——毕昇奖，被誉为"当代毕昇"。

汉字输入法的变革

现代社会中，电脑已经成为我们生活和工作中不可或缺的重要帮手。而如何在电脑中输入中文，也成了中国与世界齐头并进时需要考虑与解决的重要问题。为此，许多中国科学家编写了中文输入法，完成了中文信息处理的重要技术。

中文输入法是从1980年开始发展的。从开始的单字输入，到后来的词语输入、整句输入，中文输入法的发展可谓非常迅猛。1983年，王永民发明了五笔字型输入法，中文正式出现在电脑的输入法中。1991年，长城集团与北京大学合作推出了智能ABC输入法，通过拼音输入实现了词语的整体输入。2006年，搜狐公司发明了搜狗输入法，汉字输入法实现了长难句整句输入的高效率发展。2010年，科大讯飞设计了一款输入法，在不断完善的过程中，这款输入法集各

awarded with the "Top Ten China Scientific and Technological Achievements" and the first prize of "National Scientific and Technological Progress Achievement". He has also won the Bi Sheng Award, the highest personal honor award in the printing industry, which was set up for the first time in 1987. He is known as the "Contemporary Bi Sheng".

The Reform of Chinese Input Method

In modern society, computer has become an indispensable and important assistant in our daily life. The necessity to input Chinese characters into the computer has become an important issue that needs to be considered and solved when China and the world go hand in hand. For this reason, many Chinese scientists have compiled Chinese input methods and completed the important technology of Chinese information processing.

The Chinese input method has been developed since 1980. From the initial single character input to the subsequent phrase input and sentence input, the development of Chinese input method can be described as very rapid. In 1983, Wang Yongmin invented the five-stroke type input method, and then Chinese characters officially appeared in the computer input method. In 1991, China Great Wall Computer Group Co., Ltd cooperated with Peking University to introduce an intelligent ABC input method, which enabled the complete input of words through pinyin input. In 2006, SOHU invented sogou input method, which realized the efficient development of the input of long and difficult sentences. In 2010, iFLYTEK designed an input method which integrates all kinds of input methods and greatly improves the input speed, and has become the standard of

种输入方式于一体，大大提升了输入速度，成了当代中国智能手机中文输入法的标配，这就是十分有名的讯飞输入法。在广泛的中文输入法中，讯飞输入法因自己强大的优势成为人们的首选。

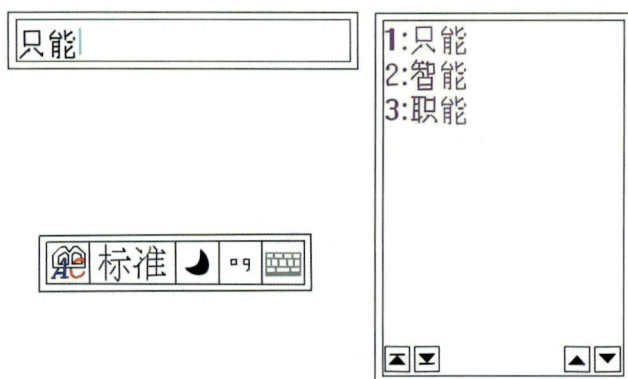

4. 重点词汇

活字印刷

谁发明了汉字的**活字印刷**?

排版

微软公司有关文字**排版**的软件是哪个?

激光

激光在现代社会有哪些应用?

输入法

中国人常用的**输入法**有哪几种?

Chinese input method for contemporary smart phones in China. This is the very famous iFLY. In a wide range of Chinese input methods, iFLY has become the first choice of people because of its great advantages.

4. Keywords

movable-type printing

Who invented the **movable-type printing** of Chinese characters?

typesetting

What is Microsoft's software for **typesetting**?

laser

What are the applications of **laser** in modern society?

input method

What kinds of **input methods** are commonly used by Chinese people?

5. 实践活动

（1）在你们国家，人们最早是用什么方法来印刷书籍的？

（2）汉字的印刷经历过五次重大的发展变革（甲骨文刻字、雕版印刷、木活字印刷、铅活字印刷、汉字激光照排）。这五次变革对汉字的字形和字体变化有哪些影响？查阅相关资料，然后和同学讨论一下。

（3）前往上海博物馆的中国历代印章馆，参观中国在雕版印刷之前的印章印刷方法，并尝试制作一个刻有自己名字的小印章，在纸上进行印制。

（4）前往上海印刷博物馆，体验雕版印刷技术和活字印刷技术，并谈谈你对这两种印刷技术的看法。

5. Activities

(1) In your country, what was the earliest way for people to print books?

(2) The printing of Chinese characters has undergone five major revolutions (oracle lettering, engraving printing, wood movable-type printing, lead movable-type printing, and laser phototypesetting). What are the effects of these five revolutions on the change of Chinese characters? Look for relevant information and discuss with your classmates.

(3) Visit the Museum of Chinese Seals of Past Dynasties to see the printing methods of Chinese seals before engraving printing, and try to make a small seal with your own name and print it on paper.

(4) Visit the Shanghai Printing Museum and experience the processes of engraving printing and movable-type printing. Share your views on them.

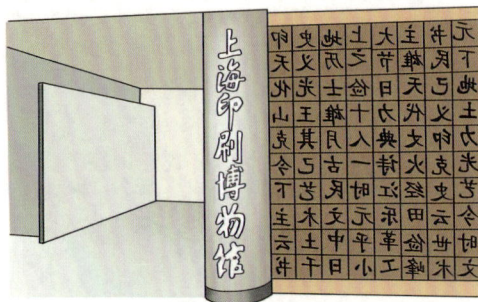

（5）分别使用智能ABC输入法、搜狗输入法和讯飞输入法写一段话，并谈谈你更喜欢哪一种输入法以及原因。

（6）你们国家最常用的输入法是什么？和中国的输入法比起来，有什么异同？

6. 自我评估

	☺	😐	☹
（1）我能说出中国古代印刷术的发展情况。			
（2）我能说出活字印刷与雕版印刷的区别。			
（3）我会使用一种汉字输入法输入汉字。			

(5) Type a paragraph using intelligent ABC input method, Sogou input method, and iFLY respectively. Which input method do you prefer and why?

(6) What is the most commonly used input method in your country? What are the similarities and differences between it and the Chinese input methods?

6. Self-assessment

	😊	😐	☹️
(1) I can tell the development of printing in ancient China.			
(2) I can tell the differences between movable-type printing and engraving printing.			
(3) I can use a Chinese input method to type Chinese characters.			

第十二课　中国传统服饰

1. 学习目标

（1）能说明旗袍的特点和发展变化。

（2）能说明旗袍受欢迎的原因。

（3）能说明中山装的名字由来和服饰特点。

（4）能说明汉服和唐装的特点。

2. 热身活动

讨论

（1）你看见过中国传统服装旗袍吗？哪里能常看见穿旗袍的女性？"旗袍"是怎么得名的？

（2）你看见过中山装吗？这个名称和哪个人有关系？

（3）你能区分出汉服和唐装吗？唐装是指唐朝的服装吗？

（4）你们国家有哪些特别的服饰？它们有什么特点？人们在日常生活中会穿这些服饰吗？

Lesson Twelve   Traditional Chinese Clothing

1. Learning objectives

(1) Be able to discuss what qipao (cheongsam) looks like and its evolution.

(2) Be able to explain why qipao (cheongsam) is popular.

(3) Be able to introduce the origin of the name of Zhongshan suit (Chinese tunic suit) and what it looks like.

(4) Be able to talk about what Hanfu (Han-style clothing) and Tangzhuang (Tang jacket) look like.

2. Warm-up

Discussion

(1) Have you ever seen the Chinese traditional costume qipao (cheongsam)? Where can you often see women wearing qipao? How did qipao get its name?

(2) Have you ever seen Zhongshan suit (Chinese tunic suit)? Who is it associated with?

(3) Can you distinguish between Hanfu (Han-style clothing) and Tangzhuang (Tang jacket)? Is Tangzhuang what people in the Tang Dynasty wore?

(4) What special costumes are there in your country? What do they look like? Do people wear them in daily life?

3. 阅读课文

旗　　袍

　　旗袍被誉为中国的"国服"。一般认为，旗袍起源于清代满族人所穿的长袍，因为满族人又称为旗人，所以，旗袍是指"旗人穿的袍子"。女子旗袍与男子的长袍有一些区别。女子旗袍的衣领、衣襟、袖口等处都镶有花边，把男袍的四面开衩改成左右开衩，下面由散大改为直筒，这样旗袍就逐渐成为女性独特的款式。自汉代起，中国汉族女性的服饰一直保持着"上衣下裳"的样式，俗称"两截衣"，穿袍服几乎只是男性的专利。而在之后几百年的发展变化中，旗袍也逐渐成为女性服装的专用名词。

　　辛亥革命后，旗袍逐渐被汉族妇女接受，并结合汉族服饰加以改进。到20世纪20年代，旗袍成为女性常穿的服装之一。此外，这个年代是中西文化交融的年代，因此，旗袍也吸收了西式服装简短的特点，不仅长度改短，而且由直筒式改为收腰式，但仍然保留了高领的特点。到

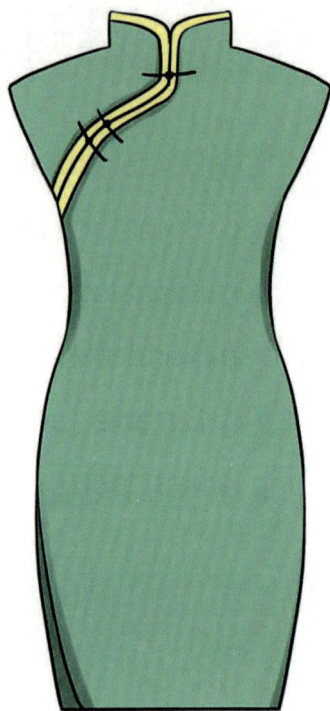

3. Reading texts

Qipao (cheongsam)

Qipao is renowned as the national garment of China. It is generally believed that qipao originated from changpao (robes) the Manchus wore in the Qing Dynasty. Because the Manchus are also called Qiren (the banner people), the name qipao refers to the robes the banner people wore. However, there are some differences between women's robe (qipao) and men's robe (changpao). The collar, placket, and cuffs of the women's qipao are all laced. There are two side slits on women's qipao compared to four slits on men's changpao, and the lower part of qipao is slim instead of the loose one in changpao. Beginning from the Han Dynasty, the Han Chinese women were dressed in a style which was commonly known as "two separated garments": upper garment consisting of *yi* and lower garment consisting of skirts called *chang*. Therefore, it was only men that had the right to wear changpao. However, after its change and modification over the next several hundred years, qipao has gradually become a term particularly referring to women's garment.

After Xinhai Revolution, qipao was gradually accepted by the Han women and developed by incorporating features of Han garment. In the 1920s, qipao became one of the common garments for women. Moreover, this happened to be the period when Chinese culture was integrated with Western culture. Taking this opportunity, qipao absorbed one feature of Western style clothing:

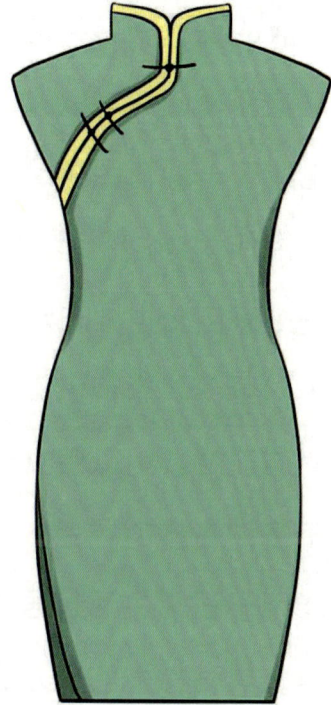

30年代，旗袍在时装的影响下，整体款式向苗条型发展。80年代，随着改革开放的深入，传统的优秀服饰再次受到女性的重视。旗袍在新的服装潮流中，又重新崛起并加以改革，人们称之为现代旗袍。90年代，旗袍更加绚丽多彩，也成了一种有民族代表意义的正式礼服，出现在各种国际社交礼仪场合。此外，旗袍作为中国服装的代表参加各种展览和走秀，在国际时装舞台上频频亮相，受到来自全世界的好评。

　　至今，旗袍仍然受到众多中国女性的喜爱。它线条简洁流畅，可以使女性的优美曲线得以展示。旗袍适用于各种各样的场合，既能用于庄重的社交礼仪场合，又能用于日常生活起居之中。旗袍又是中国文化的一种符号，具有特殊的东方美和东方神韵，也引发了电影人的创作灵感，演员在各种各样的场合中，生动地演绎着旗袍的动人形象，使旗袍这种东方服装迅速风靡全球。

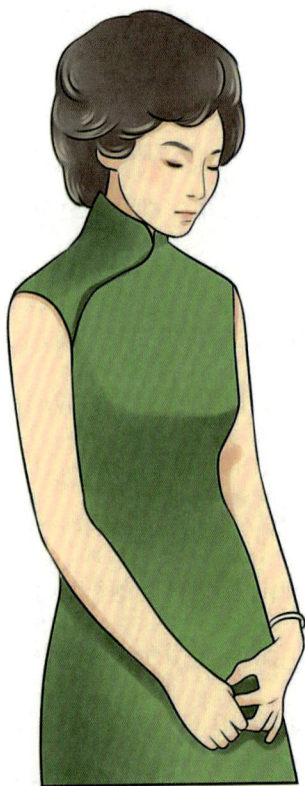

being short. As a result, not only was its length shortened, its style was also changed from being straight to being tight while keeping its high collar. In the 1930s, under the influence of fashion, the style of qipao was generally becoming slim. In the 1980s, with the implementation of China's reform and opening-up policy, some excellent traditional costumes were favored again by Chinese women. In this new fashion trend, qipao re-emerged and was reformed to become what people called "modern qipao". In the 1990s, qipao became more colorful and appeared on various international occasions as a formal dress representing Chinese nationality. At the same time, as a representative of Chinese garments, qipao was displayed in various exhibitions and catwalk shows. It appeared frequently on the international fashion stage and received high praise all over the world.

Today, qipao is still beloved by many Chinese women as its simple and smooth lines show the beautiful curves of women. Qipao is suitable for a wide range of occasions, from solemn occasions to everyday life. Having special oriental beauty and charm, qipao is also a symbol of Chinese culture, which inspires the filmmakers. Also, many actresses display the charms of qipao on various occasions, making the oriental costume popular around the world.

中 山 装

中山装是近现代中国革命家孙中山先生设计的一种服装，在广泛吸收欧美服饰的基础上综合了日式学生服装与中式服装的特点。中山装曾是最受中国男子欢迎的服饰之一。

辛亥革命后，孙中山感到西装样式复杂，而且穿着不方便，而中国传统的长衫等不能表现出中国人努力进取的精神。因此，他以当时日本流行的学生制服为基样，请裁缝设计制作了一套新式服装，把立领改为直翻领，衣服的前面开四个口袋，每个口袋上各加一个"倒山形"的袋盖，这就是中山装的基本样式。实用、方便是它的最大优点，因为口袋里可以放钢笔、书本和笔记本等，袋盖又使袋内的物品不易丢失，所以很受欢迎。现在，中山装也是中国男性的官方礼服，许多重要会议和正式场合中，可以看到身穿中山装的人们。

Zhongshan Suit

Zhongshan suit is a kind of garment designed by Sun Yat-sen, a modern Chinese revolutionist. It combines the characteristics of the Japanese school uniform with those of Chinese garment, in addition to the features of European and American clothing. Zhongshan suit was once one of the most popular costumes for Chinese men.

After the Xinhai Revolution, Sun Yat-sen thought that the Western suit was too complicated in style and not easy to wear and the traditional Chinese changshan (robes) could not show the Chinese spirit of striving to progress. Therefore, he asked the tailors to design a new style of garment, based on the school uniform in Japan at that time. Meanwhile, the "stand collar" was changed to a straight lapel, four pockets were made on the front of the garment, and a downhill shaped flap was added on each pocket, which contributed to the basic style of Zhongshan suit. The biggest advantage of Zhongshan suit is being practical and convenient. It became popular because stuff such as pens, books and small notebooks could be put in its pockets and the pocket flap could keep them safe inside. Today, Zhongshan suit is regarded as the official dress for Chinese men and could be seen in many important conferences and on formal occasions.

汉　　服

　　汉服又叫汉装、华服，是指从古代一直到明朝中原地区的人们习惯穿的服饰，统称为汉服。

　　汉服有三个基本特征，首先是交领右衽，也就是说左衣领盖住部分右衣领，因而衣襟看起来呈现为"y"字形。其次是汉服没有扣子，只是用裁剪多余下来的布料做成带子靠腋下扎起来。最后是汉服及其袖子都很宽大，弯曲身体或手臂时，会形成一个优美的线条。一直到现在，汉服仍然受到许多人的欢迎，一些年轻人会在结婚的时候选择汉服作为自己的婚装。

Hanfu (Han-Style Clothing)

Hanfu (Han-style clothing) is also called Hanzhuang or Huafu, which refers to the costumes that people in Central China wore from the ancient times until the Ming Dynasty.

Hanfu has three basic characteristics. Firstly, jiāolǐng yòurèn (cross collar and right lapel), which means that the left part of the collar covers its right part. Therefore, the lapels look like the letter "y". Secondly, Hanfu has no buttons. Instead, a sash made of leftover fabric is used to fasten the clothing under the axilla. Lastly, Hanfu has expansive cutting and broad sleeves. When one bends his/her body or arm, a beautiful line is formed. Even today, Hanfu is quite popular and some young couples choose Hanfu as their wedding clothes at the wedding ceremony.

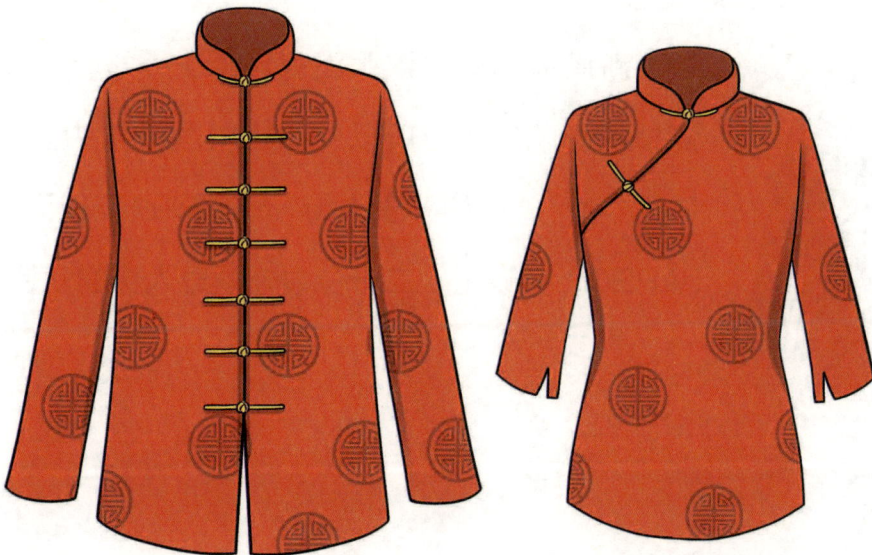

唐　装

中国有两种唐装，一种是唐风汉服，是唐朝时期在汉服的基础上改革发展而来的一种服装款式，属于汉服的一种；而另一种是以清朝满人的马褂为基础，加入立领和西式剪裁的服装形式，是传统与现代的结合，一般称为"新唐装"。

唐风汉服继承了汉服的"上衣下裳"制。中国人常说的"衣裳"在古代其实指的是两种服装，"衣"指的是上衣，"裳"指的是现在所说的裙子。唐装的上衣基本上是右衽交领或对襟系上带结，下面的裙子围起来系上长长的裙带，上衣掖在里面或者自然地松散着，外面直接套上罩衫。罩衫一般都很华丽，基本上都是拖摆至地，有的长好几米。

新唐装与唐风汉服没有任何关系，而是由于唐朝对海外的影响很大，所以外国将中国或与中国有关的事物称为"唐"，比如"唐人街"。在2001年的亚太经合组织（APEC）会议上，二十位中外领导人穿的就是新唐装。

Tangzhuang (Tang Jacket)

There are two types of Tangzhuang (Tang jacket) in China. One is "Hanfu in Tang style", which is actually a type of Hanfu, referring to the clothing adapted on the basis of Hanfu in the Tang Dynasty. Another is generally called "new Tangzhuang", which is a modified Manchu magua (horse jacket) with cutting styles of suits and "stand collar". As a combined style of tradition and modernity, it is generally called "New Tangzhuang".

"Hanfu in Tang style" inherits the traditional pattern of "two separated garments" of Hanfu, which consists of the upper part *yi* and lower part *chang*. In ancient China, the word "*yichang*" actually referred to two types of clothing: "*yi*" the upper garment and "*chang*" today's skirt. The upper garment of Tangzhuang either has yòurèn jiāolǐng (right lapel and cross collar) or its lapels are fastened with a knot. The lower garment is a pleated skirt with a long sash fastened. The upper garment is either tucked in the skirt or loosened casually. Then, a gorgeous robe is put on outside, which is usually long enough to be draped to the ground and even several meters in length.

"New Tangzhuang" has nothing to do with "Hanfu in Tang style". Instead, because the Tang Dynasty has a great influence abroad, foreigners refer to China or anything related to China as "Tang" such as "Tangren Jie" (Chinatown). At 2001 APEC, what the twenty Chinese and foreign leaders wore are "new Tangzhuang".

4. 重点词汇

旗袍

旗袍经历了哪些变化和改革?

中山装

中山装是怎么产生的?

西装

中国人一般什么时候穿**西装**?

汉服

你在中国看到过人们穿**汉服**吗?

唐装

唐装是指唐朝的服装吗?

5. 实践活动

(1)说出右侧图片中的人物所穿的服装名称。

4. Keywords

qipao (cheongsam)

What changes and adaptions has **qipao** undergone?

Zhongshan suit

How was **Zhongshan suit** born?

Western suit

When do Chinese people wear **Western suits**?

Hanfu (Han-style clothing)

Have you ever seen someone wear **Hanfu (Han-style clothing)** in China?

Tangzhuang (Tang jacket)

Does **Tangzhuang (Tang jacket)** refer to the clothing in the Tang Dynasty?

5. Activities

(1) Name the clothing the figures wear in the pictures on the right.

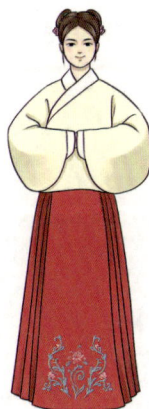

（2）日本的代表服装为和服，韩国是韩服，你认为中国的代表服装是汉服、唐装还是旗袍？请说明理由。

（3）中国的旗袍从清代之后发生了很多变化，请做一个报告，展示旗袍的变化，并且分析产生这些变化的原因。

（4）中山装的款式（比如口袋形状、扣子的数量等）都有一定的象征含义，请查找资料，说明这些含义。

（5）改革开放以后，名牌服装在中国越来越受欢迎，甚至形成"名牌热"。有些人非"CHANEL""GUCCI"等国际大牌服装不穿。你认为为什么会出现这种现象？在你们国家，有没有类似的情况？

6. 自我评估

	😊	😐	😞
（1）我能说明旗袍和中山装的特点。			
（2）我能说明汉服的特点。			
（3）我能说明唐装的特点。			

(2) Japan's representative clothing is kimonos and the Republic of Korea's is hanbok. Which do you think is China's representative clothing: Hanfu, Tangzhuang, or qipao? Please explain the reasons.

(3) Qipao has undergone many changes after the Qing Dynasty. Please make a presentation about these changes and analyze the reasons.

(4) The design of Zhongshan suit such as the shape of the pockets and the number of the buttons has certain symbolic meanings. Please look up some materials and illustrate these meanings.

(5) Since China's implementation of reform and opening-up policy, designer clothes have been more and more favored in China, which even resulted in the "brand fever". Some people only wear international brands such as "CHANEL" and "GUCCI". Why does such phenomenon appear? Are there any similar phenomena in your country?

6. Self-assessment

	🙂	😐	🙁
(1) I can describe what qipao (cheongsam) and Zhongshan suit look like.			
(2) I can describe what Hanfu (Han-style clothing) looks like.			
(3) I can describe what Tangzhuang (Tang jacket) looks like.			

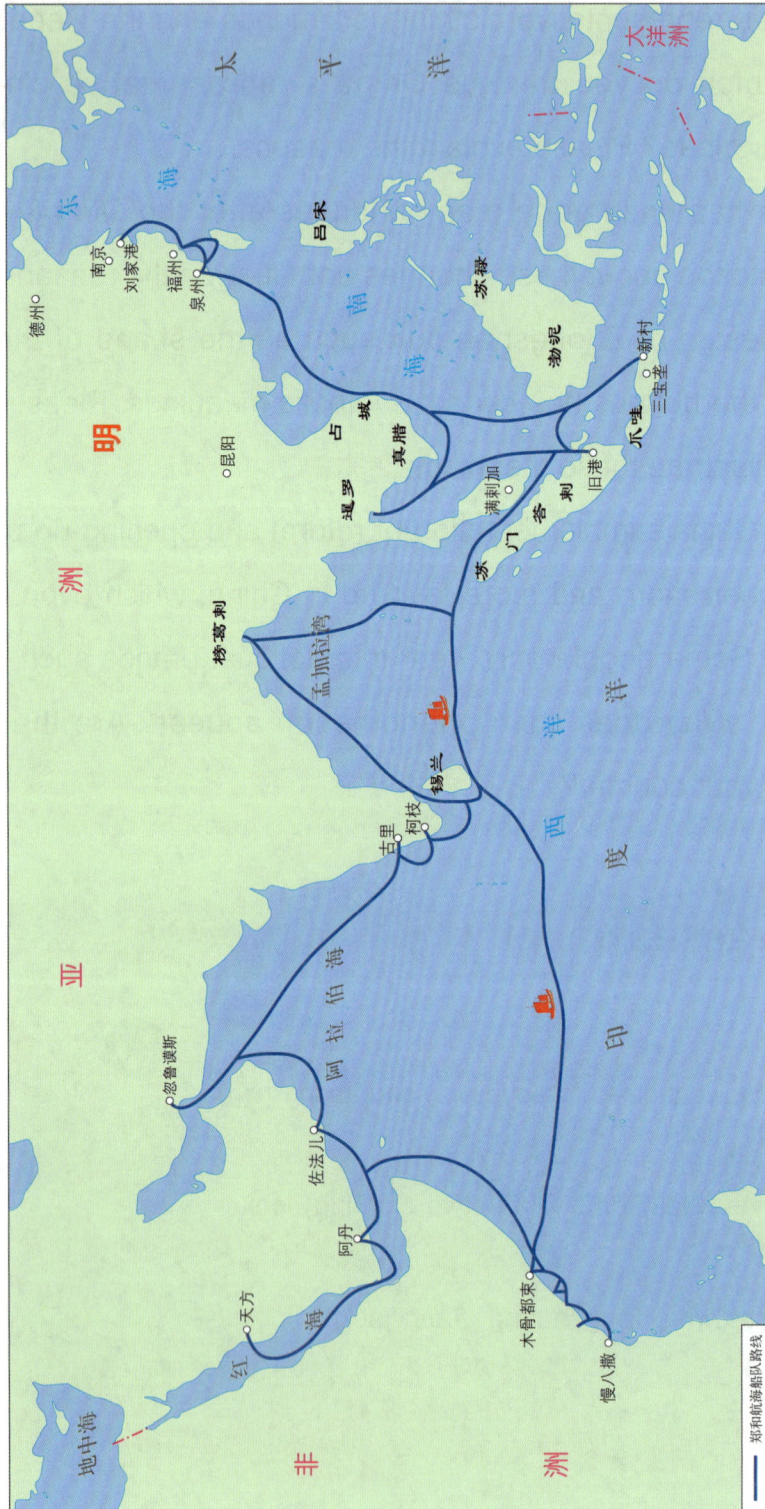

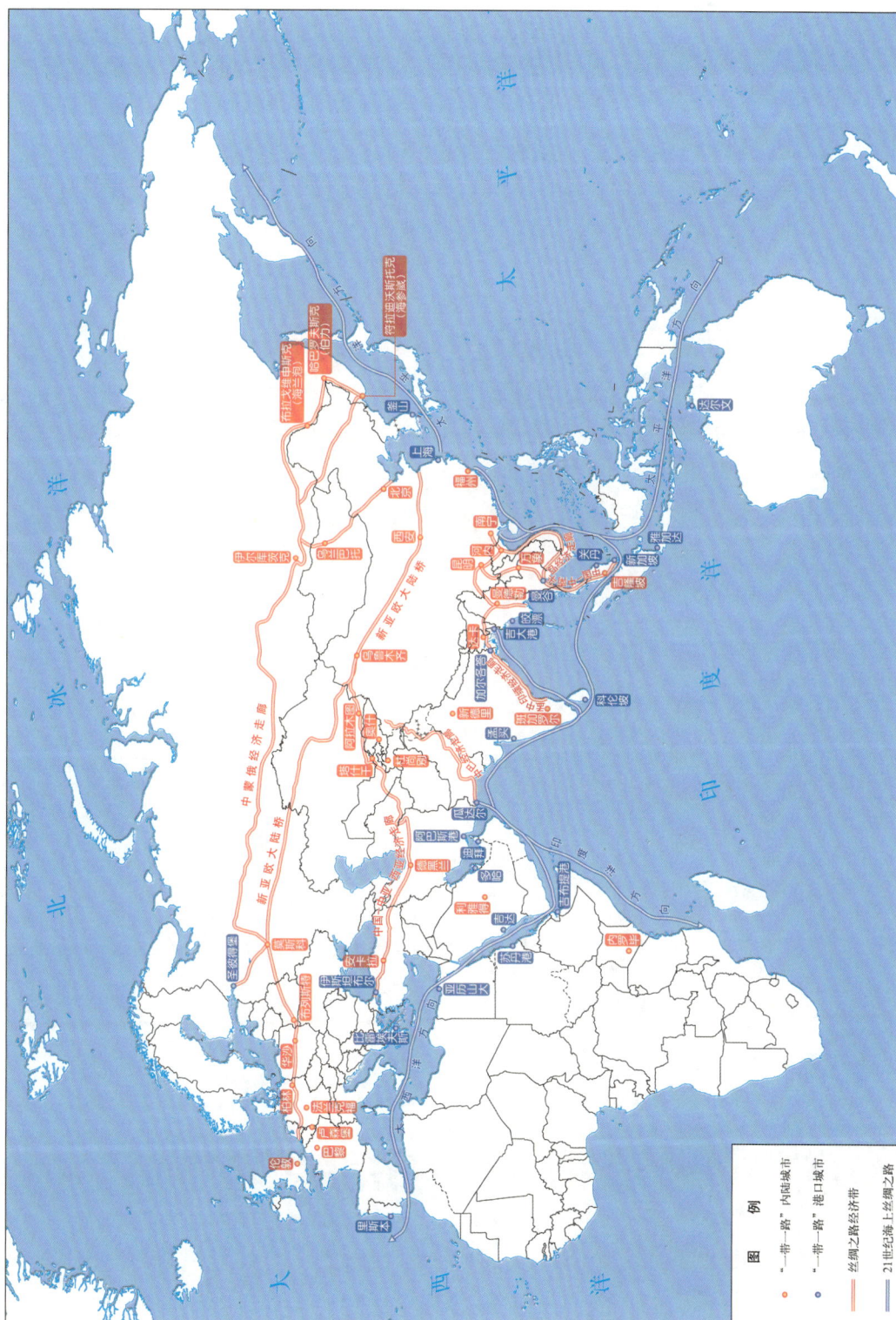